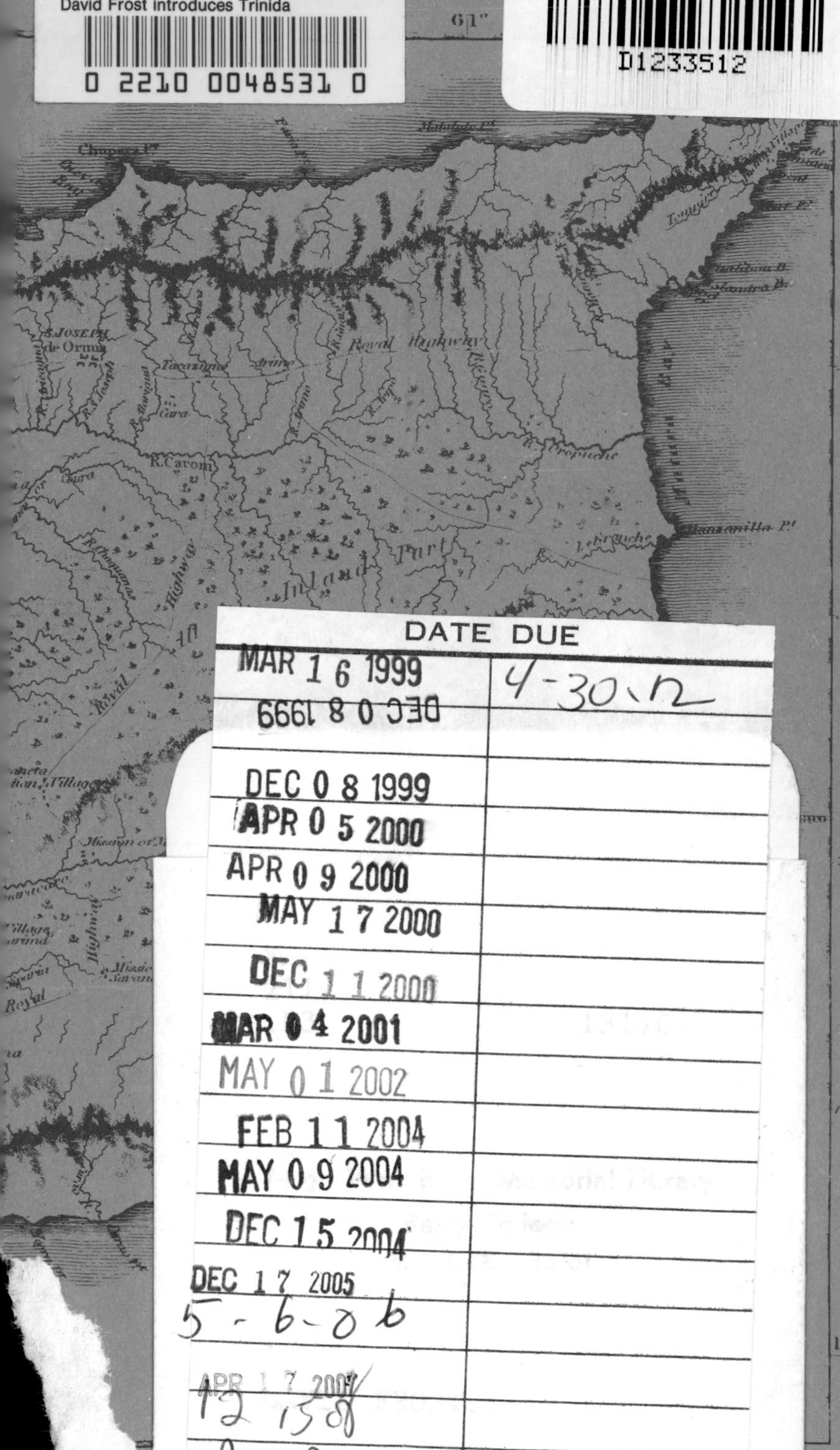
61°
Chupara Pt
S. JOSEPH
de Oruna
Tacarigua
Arima
Royal Highway
R. Caroni
Inland Part
R. Cropuche
Manzanilla Pt
40'
30'
10°

David Frost
Introduces Trinidad and Tobago

Other books in this series

Ian Fleming Introduces Jamaica
Conor Cruise O'Brien Introduces Ireland
Hammond Innes Introduces Australia
Alistair Maclean Introduces Scotland
John Kenneth Galbraith Introduces India

Books by Michael Anthony

The Games Were Coming
The Year in San Fernando
Green Days by the River
Cricket in the Road

Playing Mas'.

To Yvette and to Lucille

First published 1975 by
André Deutsch Limited
105 Great Russell Street London WC1

Printed in Yugoslavia by
Tiskarna Ljudske pravice, Ljubljana

ISBN 0 233 96274 3

The publishers are deeply grateful to the
Trinidad and Tobago Tourist Board and to
BWIA International for their help and advice.

Contents

List of illustrations

Photographs by Norman Parkinson: opposite pages 17 (bottom), 33 97 (top), 128, 144, 161 (bottom), 176.

Photographs by Noel Norton: On jacket, frontispiece, and opposite pages 16, 17 (top), 32, 48, 49, 64, 65, 80, 81, 96, 97 (bottom), 112, 113, 129, 145, 160, 161 (top), 177, 192, 193.

Introducing Trinidad & Tobago

David Frost

The first thing to remember when meeting Trinidad and Tobago for the first time is that it will be — in all probability — unlike your preconceptions. Most people seem to have two sets of these; not because there are two islands involved, but because two different images are likely to flash simultaneously on the mind's screen at the words 'Caribbean island'.

Image Number One derives from the region's holiday aspect and from gossip columnists' tit-bits about the unacceptable faces of capitalists turning brown in the West Indian sun. According to this version, sky and sea are staggeringly blue, verandahs are wide and shady, delicious-looking cool drinks are to hand. A place all *dolce far niente*, with a ripple of steelband music in the background — the perfect place in which to spend a honeymoon and perhaps even get married as well.

Image Number Two, very different, derives from the Foreign News pages of the newspapers and from political talk with black friends. A Caribbean island is a place escaped from by its sons and daughters, not because they want to leave but because it offers them few opportunities. A place of hungry minds and undernourished bodies, hovering on the brink of revolution.

The truth, I can assure you, is that although elements from both these pictures exist in most Caribbean islands, including Trinidad and Tobago, each one is amazingly different from its neighbour, and each will soon wipe out such over-simplifications simply by being itself: a real place, not a publicity hand-out for tourists or a specimen of a particular type of political problem.

I first arrived at Port of Spain by air, after a most agreeable flight with BWIA which had strengthened Image One with its comfort and efficiency, and sure enough the sky and sea were very blue. Whether the verandahs were wide and shady was not, however, immediately apparent, because factories don't have verandahs and factories are what you mostly see beside the road from Piarco Airport to the city. Slightly disappointing if you want to feel 'Here I am in a Tropical Island!', but a salutary reminder that the place has a life of its own to get on with.

My first stop was to be the Hilton Hotel, which I expected to be much like other Hiltons — they usually are. This one confounded the expectation by standing on its head. Because it's built on, or into, the side of a steep wooded hill, you enter it at rooflevel and go downstairs to your room.

I was struck at once by the friendliness of the people. It would be pointless to deny that there are islands in the Caribbean where the tourist is made to feel like an intruder, where the baleful glances outnumber the welcoming smiles, but this is not so in Trinidad and Tobago. And better still, this wasn't the bogus sort of friendliness dished out in a place primarily dependent on tourism (which Trinidad and Tobago isn't). It was relaxed, informal, inquisitive, amusing — the friendliness of people who enjoy meeting strangers. I have never, alas, been in Port of Spain during its legendary carnival, but I can easily believe it to be a marvellous experience, not only as a spectacle, but also because the revellers would welcome you into it as a matter of course.

Port of Spain can't claim much glamour, although the hills round it and the big open space of the Savannah are agreeable. But it's an easy-going place, and very open to the visitor — whatever else the Spanish part of its history has bequeathed, it's not that feeling of mysterious things going on behind high walls. It's all there to see, endless interesting and amusing details of life in a tropical city — and I would advise any visitor to spend some time in Port of Spain before making for the beaches.

I would also recommend you to drive out into the country districts of Trinidad. There are beautiful mountains to the north — with rain forest for the really energetic to explore — and the north coast, hardly developed, is superb. The gentler landscape of most of the island, largely devoted to sugar-cane is also very attractive. Mayaro, about which Michael Anthony writes so eloquently and where there are magnificent beaches, is a particular favourite of mine.

Those who spend much time in Port of Spain and make friends there will discover an extraordinarily pleasant and informal social life — and will inevitably talk politics. They will then learn that the country has, indeed, grave problems to wrestle with, but that there are any number of vivid opinions current on how they should be dealt with, and that although no one minimizes their gravity, no one supposes them to be insoluble.

Almost certainly, if you have come for a holiday and not to do business, your final destination will be Tobago. Trinidad has its oil, its sugar, its pitch, its light industries — plenty to keep it busy without bothering too much about tourism. Tobago, on the other hand, which is very small and purely rural, has little beyond its amazing beauty. Therefore, whether it likes it or not, it is becoming the part of the country to which visitors gravitate.

It's no good trying to avoid adjectives when writing about Tobago. Enchanting, magical, delicious — it deserves them all. The part of the island you see first, which slopes down and flattens out towards the little airport, is clothed in palm groves, with fawn-coloured cattle grazing in their dappled shade. Flowering shrubs, fruit trees and birds abound, the evening's catch of fish is announced by the blowing of conches, and the beaches are out of a dream. The most famous is Pigeon Point, from which you can take a boat to Buccoo Reef. There, at low tide, you hop overboard into water barely up to your waist (which feels odd at first because you are quite far out to sea), and you put on a mask more to oblige your host or your boatman than anything else, because how could such shallow water conceal anything very exciting? But no sooner are you using your mask to look into that water than the marvels appear — a sort of submarine Garden of Eden inhabited by swarms of brilliant fish quite undisturbed by your presence.

On the way back from the reef you come upon one of the minor wonders of the world: an area of perhaps a hundred yards square, at least a mile out to sea, where the water is an incredibly convenient four feet deep and feels like velvet, and covers the softest snow-white sand. It is quite simply the most memorable bathing experience I have ever known.

Other beaches, less celebrated than Pigeon Point, should be explored. On many of them the sudden appearance of Robinson Crusoe would seem the most natural thing in the world. And the forested heights of the island are as beautiful as the beaches. At first sight a forest trace looks alarming to European eyes — the ebullient tropical vegetation makes it so *very* unlike a path through a beechwood — but there are in fact no dangers, no poisonous snakes, no fierce animals.

One warning, however: I learnt by experience that if you are driving about Tobago you should pay attention to the advice given you by Tobagonians. We had driven from the charming little capital, Scarborough, along the one major road to Charlotteville in the far north-east of the island. On the way back we wanted to vary the route. 'What about that road, there?' I asked some people standing by. 'Oh no, man,' came the answer, 'That road is rugged, and if it rains ...'

We were feeling adventurous, however, so we decided to disregard this excellent advice, and we set off along the road. Almost immediately we found how rugged it was — it became a dirt track littered with boulders and there was a suspicious lack of car-tracks to be seen — but if you are feeling adventurous you want an adventure, so we enjoyed the hazards and pushed on.

And then it started to rain, and when it does that in the tropics it does it with a stunning thoroughness. The water came down not in drops but in sheets. We managed to struggle on for a mile or so, but then we came to a tree which had fallen across the road, and in our attempt to get round it we ended up in a ditch. The car was impossible to dislodge, so we started to walk — an extremely novel experience to an airline commuter. It was slightly comforting to remember that Tobago is only twenty-odd miles long, but less so to be without the faintest idea how many of those miles — five, ten, eighteen? — we would have to cover before meeting another human being or coming to a traffic-bearing road.

It seemed impossible that the rain should intensify, but it did, and we trudged on as wet as fish. After a while darkness fell, which made keeping to the already invisible track an even more complex experience. Would the going be easier without shoes? We tried without, and we tried again with — the evidence was inconclusive.

By the time we reached a road and, after plodding what seemed miles along it, saw a light, we could hardly believe it. And we were luckier than we might have been, because outside the tiny house we came to there stood an ancient jeep. We knocked at the door and asked the two brothers who answered if they would give us a lift.

Yes, they said, they would be happy to drive us home, but they weren't sure that the jeep would start because they didn't take it out all that often and it was temperamental. Still, they would have a go.

They had a go and at the third attempt, miracle of miracles, the jeep got under way. We soon found out that we would have had a long long walk if we had not met our new friends.

We talked about Tobago, its scenery, its crops, the problems and pleasures of being born, growing up and living in one of the remoter corners of a tropical paradise. Then one of our two rescuers said suddenly: 'There's one thing that worries me.'

'What's that?' I asked.

'Watergate,' he said.

'Watergate worries you?' I said in amazement — never had I felt further away from the world of Watergate.

'Yes,' he said, and off we went on that familiar discussion of the importance of the constitutional separation of powers between the judiciary and the executive.

Which, I suppose, proves that even in one of the most glorious places on God's earth in which to get away from it all, you cannot get away from it *all*.

On Choosing Port of Spain

Derek Walcott

This chapter is part of a 'planned, infinite, unfinished, casual love-letter' Derek Walcott is writing to the city of his adoption.

FOR MILDRED

I settled on this city casually
too, by a commission:
it was, like yours, my last known
refuge. I said, I would press on,
abandoning it; instead I have grown
deep in her true embodiment, a woman
with whom, as the old fall
I can, each year, recall
each landmark like a gravestone,
by Amy Bryden's house
on Fort George hill,
by seventeen blood-royalled
palms, where you as casually
sent your roots down
like fingers that befriended
other small-island dead,
while my child's burrowing head
heaves up your headstone.

Sunday morning, and the taste of coffee and tobacco increases the immediacy of Borges or Vallejo, of Hemingway or Perse to the elation of advertisements. Drink Turban Brand. Smoke Anchor. Yet by this ritual of accepting both pungencies I invent the taste of morning coffee, and the first drag, as if life itself were new. Of course it is that the morning is so mild that even its haze seems carefully filtered. It declares its promise like a novitiate. Across the mountain haze two dots, then suddenly, a dozen, somebody's gaming pigeons, are blown like scraps of paper. The pigeons are playing, like all of us, their old game of departure.

These are the mornings when it is neither elation nor resignation that accepts life, only a fine awareness of its stirrings, the nerves moving like anemones in the submarine light of The Valley, a humming which accepts the scale of things. In the house your children float on tangled sheets. You look at your wife asleep and feel that she is a woman you would like to know, and the furniture swims from dimness to a day that will have the banal clarity of water, but when you enter the study, a shared servant's quarters, with the cup of smoking coffee and settle before the altarpiece of white paper you feel as votive as others do. The pigeons also have circled and beaten back to their cotes.

Well, pardner, at forty you ent no pigeon, but you know where home is. There were friends who took you in, circling so long, with a broken wing, and you recovered here. I have lived in Port of Spain for nearly twelve years, choosing it as a fugitive collapses against a cul-de-sac, but preparing, though I did not see how, to abandon the islands. Recovery was slow but one grew to love this city before one loved one of its women. Neither have exhausted tension or surprises. Both renew themselves in sudden angles, unnerving serenities. Both have naturalized my gesture and syntax. The only defence of a small island identity is refusal to become a citizen, but the conversion is complete. I fake being an outsider, but both have made him Trinidadian. His inflections often irritate me. So is Sunday, yes.

Well, if I was a Catholic or somebody so, going to early Mass round the Savannah, or to watch the horses exercise, I couldn't love it more. But you must time it right, like all the fellers to whom horses is a religion, the right time being while the dew is still on the East Indian vendor's Valencia oranges and on bananas like the golden cast of Pharoah's hand, a carnival metaphor for this Savannah, but you have done it often enough, with wife and child, then children, and can see it any daybreak that you want to see the sweat darken a colt's flank when thc sky above Laventille is losing its rose, a sky like porcelain, with big creamy clouds that whiten quick, and imagine racing silks and the crowds. I should have kept this to myself, that it all shimmers like Lautrec or Degas, grass, horses, men and the low hills, because even if I painted what seemed theirs the truth would make it different. Different from Gauguin too, the flame trees, and the indigo foothills speckled with roofs, and from Pisarro. Too sweet, as they say here, but its true tang is acrid.

Ochres and grey-greens stipple the hills under the tower of Our Lady of Fatima, rust and orange shanty roofs below her, all shuddering back into place after the thunder of hoofmarks printed in air to the reined canter and the shaken snorting head, and this is its tang: the bite of morning in a tangerine, fresh manure and the nose-clearing smell of O, our moving Sunday breakfasts of fresh fruit. There is, ten years after that first exhilaration, the same plump East Indian woman opposite the Queen's Royal College tower slicing and salting oranges whose halves some Spanish poet has compared to a cathedral window. That acridness is the real tropical savour, hidden in sapodillas, plums, pommes cythères and pommes aracs. Any city at day-break is good. Yet none of the broken down cities in the English Antilles has her parks, none has her rhythm of the paseo whether of citizens or horses.

And in the lyrical Savannah paseo, as one hears jazz in New York streets and digging songs in Kingston, is the parang or the raga. The sitar's sinuous whine entered me for good one morning in New York when I came out of the Fifth Avenue Cinema having seen *Pather Panchali*, realising as I walked down the blurred sidewalk that it was not merely the music that had finally brought tears but a nostalgia for the Caroni plain which Bengal had so startlingly resembled: telephone poles, whitening tall grasses, canes in arrow, highways, buffalo carts, and perspectives of cabbage palms, the dark, oiled sadness in the stare of Apu, the poverty, the beauty wildly, plaintively scored by the hysterical wires of Ravi Shankar, raga on raga weaving. It was not yet my country, nor were they my race. It was not the kind of art I particularly liked, excessive sweet and selfpitying, but it

Pigeon Point, Tobago.

My Fair Lady

confirmed my exile, and my adoption. I was adrift, I had my own loss, but this homesickness for Trinidad anchored me. And since then I have preserved a nostalgia for the loss of my own India, and I wish it will widen towards all who begin here, Portuguese, Jew, Chinese and Levantine. The fear of finding Trinidad so cosmopolitan that it seemed characterless had gone.

So, somewhere, once I was being driven for my first time around the island by a lawyer friend, Bruce Procope, feeling my contempt peel layer by layer as the small-island prejudice against the country's ugliness, an ugliness, we were told, brought about by the excavations of oil, by muck-ridden East Indian villages and by barbarous, tropical boom-towns, met country that arrogantly enough began to imitate and even better the melodramatic cliffs, precipices and humming virgin forests of the greener islands. There is a silly-seeming but still admirable competition among the islanders of the whole archipelago as to which beach, which vista is the most beautiful, which is not all stupid but honourable, since no worship of nature can be evil; and its host kept smiling all through the drive, chuckling with genuine modesty when I pretended a fury that Trinidad could be so beautiful and various.

Of course there were things I had never seen, not even in the largest country, Jamaica, by which I mean those knots of Indian villages of karat straw and wattle, the hurtling and hazing avenues through the canes of Caroni, that sense of a real plain against which handsome Indian children urged mud-blistered buffaloes, the suddenly white, congealed exclamation of a mosque or a temple, with more of a sense of infinity, of India, of a continent, and, however shrunken now, of wonder then. All this is out of Port of Spain, I know, but the sense of Port of Spain is a sense of all these places, like its market smells; as on a passage along the Carenage some newly built fish-depot startlingly, almost sickeningly, evokes a longing to be alone again at Matelot or Blanchisseuse, or even the slopes behind the Hilton long for the frontier of Valencia. The city is carried a long way, like the smells of vegetable freight on one of its open trucks humming to Point Fortin or to Gasparee, and the odours stick to

Top: Hauling in fishing nets near Mayaro.
Bottom: One of Tobago's many beaches.

the flesh of memory as humidly as this sweltering, uncomfortable, piratically steamy port. You can break away, but in my sense of scale, as a smaller islander, not without a sense of effort and release, and enter at last into a thick, forested silence as if you had set out on safari. Where the sea breaks at Blanchisseuse it really tries to erase strain, and the roads, as ochre and as uncertain as those steep tracks in the real fern and liana jungles of the rain forest, really threaten with the ancestral darkness. The lamp around the hut in Naipaul's darkness attracts us all, and not with that other desolation of beaches at dusk. Moths paper the kitchen wall of the once gas-lit beach-house at Toco where the TV aerials will soon sprout, but the islandness of the national remains, and because this patois provincialism keeps the integrity of Port of Spain it has the ease of a collection of villages. Its penumbra stops at the stink of the swamp. It still has its flight of ibises at evening, which I have seen only once, coming home from the coast, but which startled like a flare, a held breath the colour of fire, a missed heartbeat the colour of the heart.

To others, understandably, a life's writing could only be variations on the theme of boredom, its variety monochromatic, as limited as the landscape's variations on green. Like Johnson's dictum on London, the man who cannot live in Port of Spain can never live in the tropics, like Blake's his sensibility must be open to minute particulars. There is an almost paralysing enervation, of course, and one can either grow fatally resigned, or be as susceptible to its weather as another literature is to the procession of seasons. The eye is sharpened to distinctions of green, to tonalities of rust and to the neutrals of weathered shingles and to overlays of flaking walls, because there is 'nothing to look at'. But living here, below impressive, changing mountains, I can feel my mind prepare for its own seasons, from dry March to rainy November, and the break in Mi-Carême, the little Lenten phase that is like a patch of washed-out sky in a rainstorm, and the sense of dereliction can take strength from changing clouds as the fisherman does from the variegations of the sea. In these suburbs I have learnt to become a lover of mountains, a watcher of clouds.

Those clouds which explode silently, like distant bomb-bursts in slow motion on the walls of raining mountains. The sun emerges, and in that glare of mist the edges of the mountain lacerate the gauze. The mountain's bulk, older than any Japanese woodcut, dissolves in the skyline (and why can't I imagine myself my neighbour, Japanese or Chinese, imagining Hiroshige or some vertical Chinese water-colour, why can't I be any other Port of Spaniard during the feast of Hosein?) as the heavy veils of the rain annihilate into essences?

Satirists, cynics, deny the tropical landscape any subtlety. They also withold sensibility from the people. They find coarseness not wit in its imagination, weight, not delicacy in this flora. They perpetuate the legend of tropical barbarity, they find our geography historiless and immature, but to some there is only one history, natural history, and anyhow below our natural history, if they want such things, there are very boring epochs of genocide and greed. Better to see every daybreak as a tentative beginning, especially in our second season, roiled and hesitant, and exploratory. The mist swallows the barking of a dog, and it crawls around the mountain huts of Morne Coco. The imagination can people it with ghosts from Asia, from India, from Africa and from Europe knowing it will chord a response from one of these peoples, and how superb if it reached them all, at once, with dew-gleaming tribal warriors from an African forest, with goat-bearded, slippered, parchment-crinkled mandarins bent under dripping willows, yes, willows, and silken waterfalls why not, with some mad woodcutter and his fear of the moon, with black samurai, and with the crude, shrill elegies of some Indian princess. All of these the mountain above our valley proffers when it is burnoosed, turbanned, kerchiefed, bandaged in vapour in the late year. It has never held these mythologies. We will never know what it held for the lost, vaporous, wailing races of the Arawak and the Carib, but we can claim them, each of us, separately, and the separations can blend with the anonymity of smoke.

Because this city is a transit station as well, a noisy ante-room between the vacation islands and the continent, someone calls up nearly every week. Some transient writer, student, even, these days, an academic preparing an anthology, an anthropologist nursing some rare thesis plucked from the islands' steam forests like a lurid botanical specimen, someone who's been given your name, and if you have him for dinner, afterwards you will show him the town. It becomes a town depending on where he is from. If you go alone with him, and it's night, you begin where he really wants to end, before rum has annealed remorse, in its shadier inns and 'hotels'.

The 'vice' of Port of Spain is somehow still ingenuous, even imitative, not quite as coarse as the wharfside houses of the smaller islands, not as sociologically explicable as the dunghill districts of Kingston or the attenuated, carefully measured lechery of Protestant Georgetown. It is quiet, corny, Hollywooden in its decor, self-conscious as a film-set. Its front is the modest beer parlour, discreetly lit, its girls gracile and solemn. To him, as host, I am showing the 'colourful' sensual side of a city that has been generous to me, not as a procurer or pimp, but to disabuse him early of 'local colour'. She remains a virtuous, or at least honest city to me, for when I first met her I was homeless and shell-shocked from the attrition of a failed marriage, and the sensual hospitality which I enjoyed was given without hope of repayment. Her character emerged in the goodness of friends, not in her reputation for avarice. So in what are supposed to be her worst, her 'rango' aspects she remains practical without being mean-spirited. Soon enough, if they remain long enough, the visitor learns that what there is to enjoy in her is not an imitation, brothel-riddled Havana of the older days, but something self-humbling, even rural. You must either accept her provincialism, her very Spanish domesticity, or give her up as dull. But one loves a city for personal reasons, not for her geographical background or her culture.

So, up to now, even writing this, I have refused to learn her history. The word 'cabildo', her Town Council in the epoch of Spanish possession, is one of the dullest sounding words, one I avoid, and I avoid hearing it as I care nothing for whatever bloody skirmishes marked the seizure of the old capital San José, nor where Raleigh knelt, nor what

Chacon did, preferring to accept her like any other small-island wetback who is tired enough of the burden of his own past. And I think that all her composite peoples feel the same, because history no longer matters. A people without this sense of the past is not necessarily lost. Is not inevitably without a purpose. There is nothing exciting about the stock-taking of merchants, and the history of Port of Spain is possibly as interesting as some Portuguese retailer's calculations on brown paper, the penny-pinching inventory of Creoles.

The Creole is the crudest alloy of the Trinidadian sensibility. To get to understand them, or it, is to shrivel vision and possibility, for the Creole mentality, which can suddenly appear in Trinidadians of every race, from any class, is the shrillest kind of hedonism, asserting with almost hysterical self-assurance that Trinidad is a paradise, that it has everything. You can find it in the false openness of some English-schooled matron denying prejudice in her life, and it exists in the same infuriating smugness that the taxi-driver displays or the fatuous calypsonians who every year in all the tents, croon that this is the greatest country on earth. It is a sort of cemented, carapaced astigmatism that can be easily put down. The first time I was flattered for being a true Creole I reacted with frightening exasperation, for the word meant to a small-islander the kind of superiority I possibly had envied and detested, privileged mindlessness.

It is a hedonism which simultaneously imitates and asserts its difference, schizophrenically capable of changing complexions, black today and part-white tomorrow, and its apotheosis is still achieved in the Hollywood-style gossip columns of our two newspapers, beginning with knighthoods and degenerating into charities, recording the latest orgies of the jet set and the in-crowd. A lost acquaintance once supplied one of our society editors with a dinner party list from *Finnegans Wake*. It is this particular boastfulness, passing for panache or a sense of the good life, that is shared by the old Carnaby Street set as well as by the saga boy and limer fantasizing his toughness, and it is a miserable failing because it passes so easily for racial pride, for communality. It is an attribute of horses, boxers, girls, water-polo players, hockey teams and politicians, it overseasons cooking, and it turns the quietest places, verandah or beach, into fete sites. Like proverbial Irish maudlin, like the proverbial wailing of Jews or the phlegm of the British, it originates in possibility, its truth being that Trinidadian, or Creole gaiety at its most exuberant can be the most depressing experience in the world. How so when its wildest display is at Carnival, 'a Creole bacchanal'?

Carnival is all that is claimed for it. It is exultation of the mass will, its hedonism is so sacred that to withdraw from it, not to jump up, to be a contemplative outside of its frenzy is a heresy. Incredibly, there are Port of Spaniards who find it repetitive, even boring in its infinite climaxes and leave the city for that weekend. But there is always one aspect at least that the heretic enjoys because it has become a myriad-faceted spectacle.

It is this ramshackle panache of both architecture and character that has made her seem self-sufficient from tourism, for up to now, piratical, opportunist, she has seen the tourist as an amusing but vulnerable figure, the self-chosen victim of taxi-drivers, vendors of hot gold watches, pimps and 'pros', but tolerable, simply another colour marshalled into the carnival patchwork of her design. Being naturally exuberant or so vigorously artificial she has never had cause to preen her wares, nor reason to isolate then market a single virtue, for that would mean analysis of her hybrid psychology, as Kingston boasts its wicked past, Bridgetown models in its nineteenth century make-up trying to be both archaic and mod, and as the truly ingenuous and beautiful islands, insisting on their beauty, have achieved the cute anonymity of fashion models in the tourist brochures. Her waterfront is a soiled, bedraggled skirt. The wharves are an industrial disgrace, and the old merchant houses are so neglected that they have the artificiality of a B-movie set.

Yet this may be because every Trinidadian black family admits with bemusement that it has small-island origins, generally Barbadian, Grenadian, or 'Vincelonian', as if these were Old World, and Port of Spain as amusedly admits this in certain small-island accents of her architecture, so that the small-island, old-world atmosphere of Belmont with its lacy verandahs, packed-tight houses, ferns and rusting roofs is pure Grenada, its coastline suburbs sound and look like the most depressed island fishing villages, so that St Peter's Chapel on the pier at Carenage, if one could leave out the bauxite terminals as if you were painting an academic watercolour, could be the fishing village of Choiseul or Canaries in Santa Lucia, while of course the greater Carenage itself, a schooner basin-mouth full of the rotting teeth of derelict hulks, barges and shallops, oblivious to the dockside machinery it hawks its goods next to as a vendor outside a new bank, with its tilted masts, ropes, wires, crates, brackish water and polyglot dialects, is Mecca to the islander sending goods home, pigs, paper-bags, vegetables, awkwardly addressed and elaborately received parcels, all full of the old, happy old-fashioned noise of the colonial ports, the boyhood days of the schooners that are so much like another home.

A Brief History

C. R. Ottley

The analysis of recent charcoal finds taken from an old midden near Penal in South Trinidad has revealed that some five thousand years before Columbus sighted the three peaks on the southern coast and christened the island La Trinidad, thousands of Amerindians* of still undertermined origin inhabited its fertile plains and verdant valleys.

Tobago, which Columbus probably never saw but which some Englishmen stumbled upon in the 1580s, was the habitat of the bellicose Carib Indians who appear to have first brought war to the West Indies. Their kitchen middens in that island have recently unfolded their story.

By the time of Columbus's arrival those early Trinidadians — the Arawaks — had erected their ajoupas all along the foothills of the Northern Range from Chaguaramas to Toco, and on the southern coast mainly around Moruga. A small settlement of those people, now of mixed blood, still live at Arima and annually hold their feast of Santa Rosa, going in procession along the streets of the town with the Carib Queen, Her Majesty Martinez the twentieth.

The original Tobagonians, however, migrated en masse some time in the eighteenth century to take up residence with their cousins in Dominica and St Vincent, and help them defend their island homes from the Europeans.

Columbus discovered Trinidad and passed on, and it was not until 1532 that the Spanish King remembered this section of his domain. At that time, the legend of El Dorado, the golden king who lived in Manoa, a city reputedly glittering with golden streets and pavements and sited somewhere on

* Descendants of the Amerindians can be found in many areas in Trinidad. Eds.

the Orinoco near Trinidad, became current in Europe. Trinidad was the natural gateway to this treasure-chest and Trinidad had therefore to be protected against other wayfarers in the search for the mythical land. The odyssey went on for some two hundred years. Gold, not colonization, was the reason for the island's original retention within the Spanish realm.

This fact was to have profound reactions on the island's development during the ensuing decades. The problem was that though its protection was vital, the extent of the Spanish domain in these parts was vast.

The King commissioned a Spanish Grandee, Antonio Sedeno, to found a settlement in 1532, but the Amerindian inhabitants drove the Spaniards out time and time again. It was not until 1592 that Antonio de Berrio, one of those early fortune hunters, succeeded in establishing the first permanent settlement at San José de Oruña, today called St Joseph.

He built a church, a jail and a town hall, all of mud and wattle, and thatched them with palm branches from the nearby forests. He set up a government — the Illustrious Cabildo — elected from among the citizens, which administered the municipal affairs of first, St Joseph, then — from 1758 — Port of Spain, when the capital was removed to that town. The Cabildo continued in being until 1840. It was a powerful body. In 1745 it rose in revolt, overthrew the Governor and put him in jail. Many of its members were later banished from the island for their part in the uprising.

De Berrio's task was formidable. He had to ward off the British, French, and Dutch corsairs and pirates. He saw his handful of soldiers cut to pieces by the British adventurer Sir Walter Raleigh, who went so far as to take the Governor of Trinidad away with him as he went searching for El Dorado up and down the Orinoco. Spain gave neither military nor civil assistance to Trinidad. A single ship visited the island each year, from the port of Seville.

~~Nevertheless~~ the first serious attempt to develop the island as a colony began in 1688, when the King sent out a number of Capuchin monks with a decree that they should subdue the Indians and convert them to the Christian faith.

Surprisingly, those Capuchin fathers who had in Spain taken the vow of poverty, found conditions in Trinidad incompatible with these vows. They not only attempted to bring their charges into the heavenly fold, but at the same time they joined the handful of Spanish planters in winning fortunes from the cocoa and tobacco plantations, the island's staples at that time. They enslaved the indigenous inhabitants in their missions. Some of these, in utter disgust, murdered three priests at Arena in central Trinidad in 1699. Later on the planters complained to the King that they could obtain no labour because the priests had taken all the Indians into their missions, and as a result a royal decree arrived ordering the Capuchins to take up their beds and go to the mainland to continue their evangilization of the heathens elsewhere.

During the eighteenth century, which began with a failure of the cocoa crop owing to a mysterious disease, life became so unbearable for the citizens that it was reported that none of them had a decent suit of clothes to wear to church, and there was neither oil for the lamps nor wine for holy communion.

While the priests were searching for fortunes in Trinidad, the English, who had long laid claim to Tobago, were busy trying to colonize it. In this task they had to contend with the Dutch who as early as 1632 had established their supremacy. They founded a township near Scarborough and called it Lampsinburgh. It contained four straight streets, a stone church, and four large warehouses where they stored the sugar for which the island was already famous.

The Dutch, however, did not have an easy time, for they had to ward off constant attacks from the French and English navies and numerous battles were fought in the island's bays and hillsides. To this day Tobago is dotted with old battlements and rusting cannons, silent witnesses of the struggles which took place there throughout the seventeenth and eighteenth centuries.

The island was even given as a birthday present by King Charles of England (he who was beheaded) to the Duke of Courland, the ruler of a small principality on the Baltic later to become a part of Latvia, and today a part of the

Soviet Union. For many decades the Courlanders maintained a settlement in that part of Tobago, which today still carries the name Courland. Death and disease finally drove them out.

During this period of her history, Tobago was a pawn on the chess boards of the countries of Europe, changing hands over two dozen times as one or other of the powers came and went.

The dispute over her reached such proportions that it was finally agreed in 1684 that the island should become a no-man's land, where all nationalities would be free to settle. As a result she became a rendezvous for the pirates who infested these seas, and stories of pirate gold are still current in the island.

Finally the English were granted suzerainty by the Treaty of Paris in 1763, and lost no time in founding a permanent settement at Georgetown near Studley Park. The development of sugar, cotton and indigo estates followed rapidly as more and more English and Scots arrived, mainly from the other islands, bringing their slaves with them.

The French returned to Tobago and occupied it on two occasions, from 1781 to 1793 and from 1801 to 1802. During this latter period Tobagonians made history when they went to the polls and voted Napoleon Bonaparte first Consul of the Republic for life.

Meanwhile, in Trinidad, the Spaniards had changed their theme of development from gold to settlement. Because they could obtain no settlers from their homeland, the King issued two decrees, the first in 1777, the second in 1783, inviting Frenchmen to come to Trinidad from the other West Indian islands, provided they were of the Roman Catholic faith.

The invitation was avidly accepted and the French came in their thousands, bringing their slaves with them, from Haiti, Martinique, St Lucia and many of the other French possessions which were in a state of ruin owing to the great revolution in France. Trinidad's population rocketed from just under a thousand in 1760 to over ten thousand by 1787. These Frenchmen, some white, some coloured and some black, busied themselves in the lucrative cultivation of sugar and cocoa.

The last of the Spanish governors, Don José Maria Chacon, whose descendants still live in Trinidad today, put a great deal of energy into the colony's economic, social and administrative life, and by the end of his rule in 1797 Trinidad had blossomed forth into one of the wealthiest islands in the West Indies, where good living was to be found on every hand. In that year there were no fewer than 468 plantations, of which 159 were under sugar cultivation. They covered a total area of 86,268 acres. It was the era of the small plantation. Trinidad soon became, as one writer put it, a Spanish colony ruled by Frenchmen, in which French traditions, language and way of life were predominant.

Prosperous though it was, the island was without organized defences. In February 1797 the British fleet, which was on its way to attack Puerto Rico, was ordered to capture Trinidad. The Spaniards were unable to fire even a single shot. The British landed and took possession of the island. The protecting Spanish navy, consisting of five ships, was scuttled by its commander Rear-Admiral Ruiz Apodoca, in the peaceful waters of Chaguaramas Bay. The English then became masters of both Trinidad and Tobago, and remained so until the islands were granted their independence in 1962.

There were many changes in both islands during the long period of British rule. While Tobago continued to enjoy a measure of representative government through its House of Assembly and Legislative Council until it became a Crown Colony in 1876, Trinidad was to be the island of experiment for Crown Colony government in which there would be no elected representative of the people until 1925. It must be recorded, however, that although England ruled supreme, the Governor in Trinidad did have a legislative body comprised of nominated and official members to advise him on the island's administration. Nevertheless, all major decisions were taken in London.

In Tobago, the abolition of slavery in 1838 brought that island's population which numbered some 20,000, merely a change from slave to free labour. In Trinidad, however, where there were barely 10,000 slaves, the sugar industry, which had undergone tremendous expansion, found itself with a dearth of hands to cultivate and manufacture the staple. Thousands of the freed Negroes left the estates to become squatters on crown lands.

Land in Trinidad was plentiful and good, capital adequate but labour short. This trio of economic circumstances was to lay the foundations on which the future of the island's ethnic, political and economic life would be built.

To fill the gap, first of all came thousands of freed slaves from the other West Indian Islands, together with many European immigrants from Germany and Switzerland and some Negroes from the United States. Then, in 1845, began the mass migration from India and Pakistan. Before the traffic was halted in 1917, approximately 145,000 of these immigrants had arrived. Thousands returned to India, one of the conditions of the contract permitting them to do so, but the majority of them chose to remain and accept the five acres of land granted to each of them at the end of their five-year period of indenture. Today their descendants comprise more than one third of the island's population.

While the production of sugar in Trinidad made rapid strides in the nineteenth century, in Tobago the position was different. The decline and final demise of sugar in that island began with the iniquitous equalization of duties of foreign and British produce in the 1840s by which the price paid for Tobago's sugar became greatly debased. There was no capital there to tide the planters over, and though they tried a system of joint cultivation and manufacture by estate owner and former slave, called the metayer system, nothing could stop the industry's decline. Some turned their lands into coconut and cocoa plantations, but this came too late to save the once flourishing island from complete economic ruin. Many Tobagonians sought sustenance by setting up homesteads on the north coast of Trinidad. Accordingly, with a revenue of only $48,000 in 1889, the island was forced to surrender its former independence and seek union with Trinidad.

Trinidad's sugar industry, on the other hand, continued to expand, fed on cheap labour and virgin soil. Between the years 1908 and 1910 the petroleum industry came on the scene, joining with sugar in giving a big boost to the island's economy.

While politically the islands were governed from London, it must be recorded that from time to time the citizens did lift their voices to press their just claims. One such occasion resulted in the destruction of the Red House (the seat of Government) by fire in 1903 and the loss of several lives. Similarly in 1937 the workers made war with Government and their employers in an effort to gain better working conditions, succeeding to the extent that they set up a chain reaction in the other West Indian islands. This particular uprising brought a new climate in the worker-employer relationship, and gave rise to the trade union movement in the country.

Agitation for political self-representation had for decades been present and increasing, and eventually resulted in full political independence on the 31st August, 1962. The country has been governed since then by the People's National Movement (PNM) headed by Dr Eric Williams.

Despite setbacks and disturbances like the Black Power upheavals of April 1970 the peoples of Trinidad and Tobago face the future confidently, vying for a dignified place in a world so transformed from that of De Berrio, Raleigh, and Chacon.

Today the country is a full member of the Commonwealth. Its representatives sit on the United Nations Assembly, the Organisation of American States (OAS), the Organisation of African Unity (OAU), and other international and regional organizations. A Governor General represents Her Majesty the Queen as Head of State. The Prime Minister forms the Government from among the 36 members of the House of Representatives and the 24 members of the Senate.*

In addition to sugar, citrus, cocoa and coconuts in the agricultural sector, many other industries have joined the flow of oil, giving employment to thousands of workers.

Local government is represented by three municipalities — Port of Spain, San Fernando, and Arima — and eight county councils — seven in Trinidad and one in Tobago.

* Reform of the Constitution, change to a republican form of government, lowering the voting age etc are being actively considered. Eds.

The Peoples of Trinidad & Tobago

Merle Hodge

The very business of choosing between 'People' and 'Peoples' of Trinidad and Tobago for the title of this chapter is charged with emotive, cross-purpose argument. Even more than the term 'West Indian', the definition of a Trinidadian is far from cut and dried.

Perhaps the epitome of a Trinidadian is the child in the third row of the class with a dark skin and crinkly plaits who looks at you out of decidedly Chinese eyes and announces herself as Jacqueline Maharaj. The strains which converge in her may be African, Indian, Chinese, French, Spanish. She speaks English — will speak standard English on occasion — but is most comfortable in a dialect of English which bears the imprint of French, Spanish, Hindi and African influences and is the common property of all her variegated classmates.

And in this dialect children will formulate racial insults:

Coolie, coolie
Come for roti,
All the roti done.

Roti is an Indian food which today forms part of the normal diet of the entire population. It is eaten with great relish by everyone, as are the Indian barah, channa, polori and aloo-pie that all schoolchildren, of any racial description, spend their pennies on. Some of the most prosperous roti establishments are run by Trinidadians of African descent.

Nigger is a nation
Damn botheration
Give them a kick and
Send them in the station.

In this chant 'nigger' is as often as not replaced by 'coolie', with no detriment to the catchy rhythm. And we have an entire racial category of African-Indian mixture, a phenomenon substantial enough to merit a new word being found to cover it — a person of mixed African and Indian parentage is called a Doogla.

Chinee Chinee
Never die
Flat nose
And chinky eye.

The Chinese, often a first-generation immigrant, from farthest afield, is the Grand Enigma. Of all the racial myths our children breathe in the air, the most fanciful are those which surround him. Inhuman longevity, diabolical eating-habits — if you miss your dog or your cat, after a week you conclude with a shrug that Chin and family at the corner-shop stewed him down for their Sunday lunch.

When one lands in Trinidad from the USA or from England, from a context of stark and simplistic white-versus-non-white racism, from a situation where the mere allusion to race is likely to offend people's delicacy, being fraught with hair-raising echoes of gas-chambers and lynching mobs, one is shocked and scandalized to find that frank references to racial characteristics are part and parcel of the normal vocabulary of altercation, on the playground as in the traffic-jam. Someone who offends you is not merely a damn fool. He is a damn coolie fool, or a damn stupid nigger, or a red ass, or a damn thieving Chinee.

Recently a little Chinese boy in my class gave a joke to the rest of the class: an Indian and a Creole (i.e. an Afro-West Indian) were having an argument — how to pronounce the word p-o-t-a-t-o-e-s. The Indian insisted the word was 'aloo' (the Hindi word for potato which has passed into our dialect); the Creole said the word was 'callaloo' (a staple Afro-Caribbean food). The arguing pair happened to pass a Chinese shop. 'Let we go in and drink a beer and ask the Chinee man.' So they went in and ordered beers and put it to the Chinee man. 'Long,' said the Chinee man, 'you long, and you long. P-o-t-a-t-o-e-s spell *pollaloes*.'

A carnival band on stage at the Savannah.

The boy's father is a 'Chinee man' — an immigrant from China. The boy is a 'Chinee-boy', but he is a *Trinidadian*, therefore sharing in the ethos of the society into which he was born, qualified to make fun of the Chinese newcomer who never quite succeeds in mastering the communal language.

There is a certain level at which we are 'a people', there does exist a distinct common denominator of consciousness or culture. But an important aspect of this collective consciousness is our awareness of racial and cultural diversity, the awareness that our society is composed of several different *peoples*.

Racially, and by the same token culturally, Trinidad presents the Caribbean in microcosm. The other islands are more homogeneous in character, or at least strongly marked by a particular influence. Barbados is Little England, Martinique is unmistakably French, Haiti has preserved an essential Africanity and there are Spanish islands. In Trinidad all these cultures are represented. There is the Britishness of Trinidad — English is our official language, our legal system and constitution are British. There is the French Creole presence — French patois is still a vigorous language in the country, a large number of our folk-songs are in patois, our English dialect is strongly flavoured by patois. African culture survives in many areas of our daily life — in our music, our food, in our indigenous religions, Shango, Obeah, Shouters and other sects in which a synthesis of African and Christian elements is effected. Spanish influences are abundant — the language is still spoken in some parts of the island, many of our folk-songs are in Spanish; parang, our Christmas music, is Spanish. Our proximity to South America (the Venezuelan coastline is visible from Trinidad) makes for continuing Spanish influence.

Almost all the races present in the Caribbean are to be found in significant numbers in Trinidad, whereas there are islands from which certain of our peoples are practically absent. The Indian population of the Caribbean is almost entirely restricted to Trinidad and Guyana, although there is a sprinkling of Indians in other islands. The Chinese are a significant presence in our community, but less so in other

Impressions of carnival.

parts of the Caribbean. There is even a handful of Caribs* in Trinidad, when this, the indigenous race of the region has died out completely from most of the other islands.

A sampling of our place-names will help to illustrate the permanent impact which the various peoples have made upon the country. Although the Amerindians have all but died out here, the names they gave to their settlements remain. In the most literal terms the Carib is buried at the four corners of the rectangular island of Trinidad. One of Naipaul's characters frames the notoriety of a certain goat: "'Everybody in Trinidad who know about goat know this goat, from Icacos to Mayaro to Toco to Chaguaramas," said he, naming the four corners of Trinidad.' The Amerindian names are many-syllabled and lovely to pronounce, and flavour the everyday vocabulary of all the peoples who have inherited this piece of Carib soil: Guayaguayare, Cunaripo, Chacachacare, Caroni, Naparima, Tunapuna, Carapichaima, Mucurapo, Tamana.... The Spanish name 'Trinidad' (Trinity) was given by Christopher Columbus; Spanish settlers named Santa Cruz, Rio Claro, Sangre Grande, El Socorro, San Fernando, Manzanilla.... Some of our French place-names are Pointe-à-Pierre, Blanchisseuse, Champs Fleurs, Bonne Aventure, Grande Rivière.... Many an English town has its namesake on the island of Tobago, — Scarborough, Plymouth, Roxborough, Pembroke — but in Trinidad the English place-names are a minority scattered among the place-names given by the other peoples. African place-names, however, are even more rare: the African worked the land for centuries without ever owning one jot of it. Indian indentured labourers, on the other hand, were given grants of land as an inducement to stay. Fyzabad, Hindustan, Calcutta Settlement, Madras Settlement, Cawnpore Road, are among the places named in tribute to India.

Catholicism is the majority Christian religion, reflecting the island's Spanish and French history. The Church of England takes the next largest share of the Christian popu-

* Whether there were Caribs among the Amerindians of Trinidad is a matter of controversy among experts. Eds.

lation, but almost every important sect of Christianity is vigorously represented. Fundamentalist religion has a strong appeal as it tends to accommodate some characteristics of African religions. The Indian population is mainly Hindu or Muslem, but a number of Indians have been christianized, mainly by the Presbyterian Church.

Racial rivalry and disaffection exist, despite the sentimental inaccuracies we publish about ourselves in the tourist brochures. History has cast the various races in certain roles, and this, along with the inevitable differences in attitudes, inclinations and ideals from one group to another, leads to racial stereotyping.

The labouring classes are African and Indian, but there is a certain mistrust between them. The African is alarmed at what he sees as phenomenal progress on the part of the Indian, the 'coolie' who was imported to occupy the ignominious lowest rung of the society vacated by the African at Emancipation.

It is said that the experience of slavery-forced labour on the plantations bred in the African an aversion to working the land. The Indian has certainly remained closer to the land than he. Indians introduced rice to the Caribbean and continue to be responsible for its cultivation, and the sugar-cane belt is populated mainly by Indians. So to the rest of the population the 'coolie' belongs down in Caroni or Chaguanas, ankle-deep in a rice-patch, or bundling cane, and seems threatening when he turns up elsewhere. Traditionally the African's ambition has been to move into white-collar jobs, the professions. Today the Public Service is still manned mainly by Africans. But more and more Indians have entered the professions and as many Indians as Africans are qualifying for scholarships to higher education: yet there is still the feeling that the Indian with a University degree is an upstart, an impostor: 'He still ain't nothing but a coolie man.'

Most alarming of all to the African is the Indian's commercial activity. A new character has slipped into our folklore: Ram the barefoot Indian selling penny packets of channa outside the school, and his penny-channa miraculously building up in a few years' time into an island-wide 'empire' of shiny hardware stores. Ram is a most treacherous figure.

The African meanwhile chastises himself for his lack of 'business sense', for his slackness in letting the 'coolie' creep up on him. No one subscribes to the caricaturization of the African as much as the African himself. He will tell you cheerfully that his people are no good at anything, that every other race will overtake them by their industriousness while they drink rum and dance, sing, play mas' and dress to kill.

But there is little penitence in this self-chastisement. The African is contemptuous of the Indian's values, he abhors his asceticism, sees no point in a life-long thrift the fruits of which he may only reap in his infirm old age, or perhaps never at all, for often it is a succeeding generation which benefits. The same holds good for the African's attitude to the Chinese.

Another cause of mistrust between Africans and Indians is the cultural tenacity of the Indian. The Indian arrived with his culture intact — his gods, his name, his language. Despite creeping westernization, the core of his culture remains, an indissoluble factor in our midst. The total disruption of the African's culture has left him pliable, given him a chameleon nature, made him a man without fixed values. So that the Indian who remains stubbornly Indian is an opaqueness with which he cannot cope, an unknown quantity he cannot reckon with.

The African often accuses the Indian of 'clannishness', which only means that to him the Indian is too inward-looking, too self-sufficient, in contrast to his own openness and receptivity. In fact the African, the ex-slave, has traditionally sought to escape from his racial classification, to belie his African origins and move 'up' into whiteness. It is only within the past decade that he has begun to perform a *volte face*, fairly erecting his africanity into a religion.

It is too easy to dismiss the 'Afro' movement in Trinidad as merely another fad imported from America. Of course there is some posturing and fad-following, but basically the new glorification of blackness, the wearing of African fabrics and of clothes inspired (at an obvious distance) by traditional

African styles, the displays of African hair that would have been considered obscene ten years ago — all of these manifestations illustrate the ex-slave's thirst for the restoration of his manhood, for an authentic manhood, defined by himself and not by the criteria of his masters.

The single phenomenon of young men wearing their hair in plaits is a gesture which contains more defiance and self-assertion than can adequately be conveyed to thc outsider.

Hair-plaiting, which is the natural form of hair-dressing for the African woman, has been frowned upon in the West Indies as a 'niggery' habit. It was only used to tame little girls' hair. Traditionally the African woman in the Caribbean made herself socially acceptable by straightening her hair and fashioning it into European modes, while the man suppressed his hair — kept it shorn low and inconspicuous. So that today's gesture of allowing a man's hair to grow abundantly, re-instating hair-plaiting for women as an accepted mark of beauty, and then going one step further and decreeing that it shall be acceptable for the African male in Trinidad and Tobago also to wear plaits if he so desires, is a complete reversal of Afro-West Indian servility to other people's norms.

Fortunately the political creed which accompanies the Afro movement insists on a reconciliation of the two major races of Trinidad, invoking their common dispossessedness, so that it does not in itself contain the threat of Afro-Indian confrontation, as might have been feared. Instead it proposes (but so far with no remarkable success) their welding into a common front against a common oppressor who is still identified as white or fair-skinned.

Why is this, ask Europeans, when the country is now run by black people? But a light skin remains a passport to privilege. It is an unwritten requirement for positions of greatest responsibility in big business, and for other areas of employment which carry a certain social status. Bank clerks, secretaries or receptionists in large firms, or clerks in the more prestigious department stores are usually the descendants of the mulatto who since slavery was considered closer to human than the pure African.

In the crudest terms, ownership is still white (expatriate or native-born), and dispossession still black, despite those blacks who may have strayed up into the fairer income brackets.

If the tourist brochure's idyll of diverse peoples living in harmony is to begin to be a complete reality, there are two important currents of racial disharmony to be dealt with. One is lateral: the Afro-Indian tension, a double current; and the other runs vertically, from top to bottom. Given the economic strength of the white minority it seems absurd to speak of this vertical tension in terms of black 'racism' against whites; like feeling sorry for the elephant who complains of some ants in his path looking up at him with resentment.

But then, of course, the ants will never conceive of manufacturing Molotov cocktails. And this, presumably, is what leads the powers that be to introduce alarmist legislation to forestall 'genocide'. In the violence of 1970 our society was able to measure the resentment of the dispossessed against the owners; the dividing line is conveniently laid down by history, black on the one side, white on the other. The black man had no part in drawing this line, and to treat the resentment that black feels against white as 'racism' pure and abstract is to attack the phenomenon from the wrong end.

In the long run, however, the 'vertical' current of racism in our society will not be the most significant. It rests on economics and when its economic foundation is removed it will cease to matter what one per cent Whites thinks of eighty per cent Blacks.

Afro-Indian disharmony is potentially more worrying. Continued prejudice between these two major groups would be more devastating to the society.

Here again economics enter into the problem. It is extremely dangerous for a multi-racial society to entrust its progress so emphatically to the principle of competition, for it means that all the other factors which contribute to racism — factors which appear to be instinctive and are hard to pin down — find a ramping-ground in such competition. Africans and Indians are at loggerheads not merely because they differ somewhat in appearance and customs, but because they think in terms of the one stealing a march on the other to get a bigger share of the cake. Economic competition gets mixed up with race, and becomes racial rivalry.

One obvious weapon against racial prejudice at the primitive or emotional level is education. But for the time being in Trinidad and Tobago African and Indian citizens come up through the school system with their myths about each other intact.

There are those who see our salvation in a consciously implemented levelling-out of the races in cultural terms. But this, precisely, is one of the causes of tension. Each group periodically accuses the other of wanting to impose *its* character, of wanting to swamp the other's individuality. Africans often complain of the quota of radio time given to Indian music (about two hours a day out of a total of eighteen broadcasting hours), and shiver to think of what would happen if an Indian political party came to power (traditionally, political parties have tended to form themselves along racial lines), for then 'they' would surely go the whole hog and make this a 'Coolie country'. An Indian rebuke, usually aimed at a member of the younger Indian generation, is 'You getting too much like nigger!'

Cultural pooling, voluntary and unforced, rather than cultural levelling out is what is to be desired. And already, almost imperceptibly, Africans and Indians have begun to adopt what they will of each other's culture. They participate freely in each other's festivals and cultural manifestations. Indians invite their African neighbours to share in the feasting of Divali and Eid (respectively a Hindu and a Muslem religious festival, each a public holiday in Trinidad and Tobago). The dialect spoken by all Trinidadians was fashioned originally by the African slaves and their descendants. Indians have begun to beat steelband and compose calypsoes (both originally African developments), as Africans now beat drums in the Indian festivals of Phagwa and Hosay, and Africans have taken to mastering Indian dances.

This stealthy interlocking of our cultures, this consummation of our personalities, is very promising. It is wrong to demand that the Indian make a deliberate effort to abandon his character in the interests of racial reconciliation; neither is the African's new racial consciousness to be seen as a threat to racial harmony. Just as a truly civilized individual is one who has achieved the balance involved in being true to himself with no detriment to the interests of his neighbour, so as a society we shall have attained to a rare degree of civilization when the rich diversity of our racial and cultural characteristics implies no conflict with the fact of our being a people.

First Sight

Diana Athill

Mangrove swamps: words which used to sum up the steamy glamour of the tropics but which now suddenly meant some spinach-green woods on the edge of the sea passing under the aeroplane. I could distinguish one big tree covered with white specks. The specks scattered out from it and settled back. Birds — *egrets*! I'd heard of excursions from Port of Spain to see the scarlet ibis in the Caroni swamp, and knew that although the ibis are the big draw, there are egrets too. They, in their whiteness, would be the ones visible from high up. 'A flock of egrets in a mangrove swamp'; it sounded so exotic, but all it looked like from up here was pigeons in an oak wood.

Most places look ordinary from the air because colour and detail can't be picked out. This pleases me because places *are* ordinary. To the man who has a mango tree and hummingbirds in his yard all his life, mango trees and hummingbirds are as ordinary as apple trees and chaffinches are to me; and what I long for when I travel is not marvels (although I enjoy them when they come) but a feeling of what it would be like to belong to this place. The remoter the place, the more interesting the nature of its ordinariness, and I like the 'disappointments' of arrival — the scruffy terrain round an airport, the factory buildings on a road into a city — because they suggest this.

Trinidad's airport provides plenty of ordinariness. There is no startling feeling of 'abroadness' until you are nearly in Port of Spain; but then, if you are on the upper road, you see a panoramic view of city and sea which couldn't possibly be Portsmouth or Atlantic City.

I began to feel the island's beauty even more strongly when I reached the suburb where my guest-house was.

'Suburban' is a drab adjective, but the better-off suburbs of Port of Spain are anything but drab. The gardens are like overspill from the magnificent forests which cover the mountains of both Trinidad and Tobago (walking in Tobago, later, I realized I had seen those forests before in the paintings of the Douanier Rousseau). The gardens flame with flowers and are thick with a fascinating variety of delicate or dramatic foliage. There were a lot of birds about, too (though later some of the squawkings and flutings turned out to come from frogs, and some of the swooping and flitting to be done by bats), and the chirring of insects was constant. Of all these voices the '*Qu'est ce qu'il dit?*' of the keskidee — the most appropriately named bird I know — was the most insistent, and was to become Port of Spain's 'signature' in my mind. The guest-house was only a few minutes from the centre of the town but it felt lazy and rural. It looked out across a valley full of embowered houses to the wooded crest of a hill behind which the sun went languidly down while house and street lights came on haphazard and starlike. On my first evening I felt the journey would have been worth it if I did nothing more than sit on the terrace with a cold drink, watching this scene and absorbing the fact that here nightfall didn't mean chill, but only an easier and more delicious warmth.

People — travel agents and so on — may try to persuade you that there is nowhere to stay in the Caribbean but swish hotels at which you have to book a year in advance. No doubt they are right about the booking, and I was uncommonly lucky in getting away without doing so, but if you are inclined towards smaller establishments don't let anyone convince you that good ones don't exist. I took a chance in Port of Spain and found this pleasant, well-run and friendly guest-house; and I took another in Tobago and found what I now think of as my favourite hotel. Both were small places, and cheap by Caribbean standards (which doesn't mean cheap by European ones).

I can't claim that the guest-house was quiet. I doubt whether anything is in Port of Spain — light sleepers should take ear-plugs. Apart from the birds, frogs and insects there were the cocks and the dogs. Port of Spain dogs don't bark only when there is something to bark *at*; they just bark. And Port of Spain cocks, like those in Greece, crow all night as well as all day. Add the occasional donkey, a lot of human voices and a great many radios, and you needn't be in a neighbourhood where a steelband practises to be in a noisy place. But noises made chiefly by animals and people communicate something and can grow on you. On reaching New York immediately after leaving Trinidad I found myself longing for the sounds of Port of Spain and thinking fondly even of the dog who lived two houses down from the guest-house, whose bark had been more fatuously persistent that all the others.

Heat should be taken for granted in a tropical country, but to an English visitor escaping winter it is such a luxury that it has to be mentioned. The open style of life it favours, the freedom of shedding all but the lightest clothes — heat is *release*, and it conditions social behaviour in a wholly agreeable way. No one is pompous or formal in Trinidad and Tobago, because no one can bear to wear pompous or formal clothes and everything that can happen out of doors rather than indoors does so happen. To start with the northerner hates to sweat, but although the consequences of any sudden or unusual exertion are certainly dramatic, you soon learn that sweat evaporates fast in great heat. Once you have relaxed and accepted the climate it becomes delightful.

For the first few days it may make your feet swell, and they will swell even more if you arrive during the carnival, as I did. I heard someone say that no one has yet invented the right shoes for jumping up (the local expression for dancing), and they haven't. I recommend several pairs of the lightest and most open sandals, each of a different design so that when one set of straps starts chafing you can change to another which chafes in a different place. Carnival is described by Andrew Carr elsewhere in this book so I shall only say that my expectations were great and were made puny by the reality. If you can time your visit to include the carnival, do so: it comes high in the category of marvels.

It is not only the suburbs which have a rural atmosphere. The Savannah is more like an immense village green than an urban park, and countrified things go on even in the business and shopping centre of the town. There are villagey houses tucked between office blocks, and almost everything is shabby. The new shabbiness is ugly; the old is often made pretty by gingerbread (wooden fretwork) and wrought-iron. Some of the balconies are very beautiful, and a good many houses beside 'the Magnificent Seven' on the Savannah (see John Newel Lewis's chapter) have a mad, fairy-tale charm. The climate encourages indoor and outdoor life to merge and flow together in the streets, and the pace is leisurely. Brisk business must often be done in this town, but it is rarely seen to be done.

Port of Spain is not elegant, not prosperous-looking, not spectacular — so why did I like it at once? Because, I think, it is still shaped by and for people, not machines (something which drivers caught in its traffic jams — and those *can* be spectacular — must fail to appreciate). The people — this is important — still bother to look at each other. You are inspected as you pass, almost always politely, but even if a glance is critical or ironical it is better than the gooseberry-eyed indifference of a northern city. And casual contacts are likely to be amiable. People in Port of Spain sometimes reminded me of the Irish: great talkers and holders of opinions, who make the maximum conversational use of the information at their disposal. It is hard to identify the ways in which a people's characteristics make themselves felt, but I know that after a week or so I had become less surprised by the creative energy displayed in the carnival; and I was less surprised, too, that political ferment should have gone further here than in other places where its causes are even more apparent.

That some — not much — of this ferment has been overtly hostile to whites, may have discouraged some would-be visitors. It is felt throughout the Caribbean that the foreign investor does better out of the region that the region does out of him, which is true, and occasional racist manifestations are bound to appear when this uneasiness comes to the boil; but judging by my own experience I conclude that racism goes against the grain with most Trinidadians and Tobagonians. The visitor can usually expect an engaging welcome. In small places strange faces are usually seen as more interesting than tiresome. They are gossipped about, of course, if they give the least grounds for it (and Trinidad gossip is likely to be salty), but they are enjoyed.

There were times when it struck me that Trinidadians and Tobagonians must be exceptionally mellow and forgiving people to put up with their visitors so graciously and to take them for so few rides. They take them for some, naturally enough, but not many considering what an ostentatious 'have' the average tourist is in a country of many 'have nots'. It is not blameworthy for a visitor to want a holiday to be simply a holiday — a period in which he relaxes in maximum comfort, enjoying his swimming or his golf against a beautiful and exotic backdrop provided by a foreign country (something which Tobago, especially, with its ravishing beaches and magnificent golf-course,* provides to perfection) — but it does insulate him from the people in whose country he is taking his holiday, to whom the beautiful and exotic backdrop is the place where they live, many of them in circumstances almost unimaginably remote from the visitor's. A Law of Tourism: the man who sees the native not as a person but as a part of the scenery is viewed by the native not as a person but as an opportunity for profit, and this law operates in Trinidad and Tobago as it does everywhere else. But everyone I met who had approached the place naturally had been taken naturally in return — or had even been slightly overvalued by his hosts, which was a sad comment on the majority of visitors.

The way to see Port of Spain as a city rather than as an overgrown country town is to go to Tobago and look at it from there. There can be few islands in the world more lovely than Tobago, and I made friends there who filled its loveliness with warmth, but it's no use pretending that it isn't quiet (for which heaven be praised!). In Tobagonian eyes Port of Spain is a glittering and risky metropolis where you have to look sharp among all those over-clever and

* This is one of the most beautiful golf-courses in the Caribbean. It was designed by John Harris and is part of a wider project including a luxurious hotel and a number of private housing sites available for sale.

disreputable townees. In Tobago you are being pretty reckless if you are not in bed by eleven (you are far too drowsy from sun, sea and beauty to mind this), and a young friend of mine who wore a mini-skirt when she came over from Port of Spain to visit her grandmother in Scarborough was all but disowned, so no great intensity of urban vice is needed to raise Tobago's eyebrows. But it was interesting to discover that Port of Spain *was* more raffish when I got back to it. Someone advised me not to walk alone at night, and whereas before I would have laughed, now I looked around me and thought 'Well, yes — it *is* after all a sea-port, and there are a lot of people in it who have only their wits to live by.' And there was a kind of swagger about it now ... but the fact remains that it still failed utterly to feel threatening. A bit raffish, yes; more lively than I'd thought at first (except during the carnival, which was electric from start to finish); but still much more easy-going and friendly than many cities of my acquaintance.

And small. The whole country, all two islands of it, is small. To those who live there this must often be extremely frustrating (at the most frivolous level — how, I wondered, does anyone ever manage to seduce his/her neighbour's wife/husband without everyone's knowing?); but it is a great advantage to the visitor. He only needs to make one or two friends, and he is able almost at once to begin knitting the threads of current gossip into a pattern, to pick up passing references, to understand jokes, and to feel surprised if he doesn't meet so-and-so at such-and-such an occasion. I was soon feeling it *odd* when I didn't bump into someone I knew when I was pottering the streets on a shopping expedition: surely I would in a moment! This place was the furthest I had ever been from England, and the most unlike it, but I had already, in an absurdly short time, acquired the illusion of being at home. It *was* only an illusion, of course, but it was a harmless one, and very seductive: quite as seductive as the sun, the incomparable sea and those Rousseauesque forests. Trinidad and Tobago had given me, it turned out, exactly the experience I most enjoy: it had allowed me to feel, however dottily, that I belonged there.

It must have been this gift which made leaving so sad. I have left a lot of places with regret but none with such a sharp sense of loss, and when I peered down from the aeroplane for a last look at the mangrove swamps, they had changed. They were still unlike the fanciful image of anticipation, but they no longer made me think of oak woods. They had become ordinary old mangrove swamps: part of a place which I loved and to which I would certainly return as soon as possible. It seemed to matter a lot that I should hear that plaintive cry of '*Qu'est ce qu'il dit?*' again before I was done.

In a South-eastern Village

Michael Anthony

The grunting bus comes down the main road and stops where the road ends, at Plaisance, just in front of the sea. There are voices in the darkness and it is clearly the voices of the passengers. The sound of the bus engine stops, but the voices of the passengers continue, until somebody says, 'It's five o'clock, oui!' which here is simply saying that it is five o'clock. The French 'oui' at the end of the sentence just means 'yes'. This does not fall strangely on the ear, for we are in patois-speaking Mayaro, deep in the heart of the South-East Trinidad countryside. The bus then starts up again and turns and takes the long road to Rio Claro, another country village about 14 miles in the interior. It will make this trip several times during the day, but this is its first trip, and as it grinds its noisy way through the village everybody in the roadside houses knows that it is five o'clock. But this is not their only time-piece for they also have the chant of the cocks. The cocks have already crowed, answering each other across the hills and under the palms, and will crow again presently, for it is near daybreak. It is still pitch-black, although over the Atlantic there is a clear patch promising the appearance of the sun. The birds are already beginning to twitter wildly in the branches of the coconut trees; the leaden sea and the distant headlands are beginning to appear. One more day is about to dawn on the Mayaro countryside.

Shortly after the cocks chant for the third time, the day shows that mixture of light and darkness which the people at Mayaro call 'fore-day morning'. Now on the beach one can see the row of coconut palms which run thickly along the coastline. One can also see the houses under the palms — the great, luxurious ones, which are holiday beach-houses, and

Ambard House, now Roodal's Palace: detail.

the modest little wooden ones, which are the dwellings of the beach-folk. Looking back towards the sea, now a sheet of silver in the dawn with the sun just glinting above it, one can see the headlands clearly, and the turbulent water that is Mayaro Bay.

Even while one is looking at the sea one can hear low chattering, and on looking back, one can see the black, shadowy figures underneath the palms. These are the Mayaro fishermen. All along the coast, beside little dwelling-houses, there are boats — either covered with coconut branches, or in little boat-houses, and it is these boats that the fishermen are now preparing to push across the wide beach to the sea. This is not an easy task for the twenty or so men, for the stern of the boat is piled high with seine — fishing net — and the boat itself is huge and the sand is loose. But the fishermen do not delay. They have an accurate time-piece in the sun, and some of them are probably looking at it now and saying something like, 'Come on, man, it's nearly six o'clock, oui!' Only this time he might speak in French patois, the dialect he prefers.

The boat is pushed down to the water in short, sharp heaves, and to the chanting of some old patois seine-song. The chanting gives the signal to push, to rest, and to push again, and the fishermen heave and push and are so cheerful that they do not even feel the burden. So in no time the boat is at the water's edge, and now the fishermen just have to wait for the little shore-waves to lift the boat a little off the sand, which will make the pushing much easier. As soon as the boat begins to float and get into deeper water, two or three of the men jump in and begin to help it seaward with their oars. As it begins to hit the breakers the rest scramble in, leaving a few companions on the beach to 'follow' the boat.

By the time the sun clears the sea, dozens of boats dot Mayaro Bay. By this time, too, the coast has awakened to life, and one can see fireside smoke billowing from the houses under the palms. The coconut climbers are beginning to be active too, and there they are under the palms, with cutlasses in hand, and big, circular, climbing-ropes, ready to walk up coconut trees; for here, on coastal Mayaro, man does not

Boissière House, Port of Spain: characteristic architectural ebullience.

live by fish alone. The little factories at intervals on the coast need the kernel of the coconut for making coconut oil and copra, and for making stock-feed, like oil-cake, and they need the fibre for making mattresses. Therefore the coconut palms with their fronds waving in the breeze are not just ornaments of this Atlantic Coast, but a vital part of the livelihood of this village.

Mayaro is not all coast. It is a number of little seaside settlements, like Plaisance, and inland settlements like Pierreville. Pierreville, called 'Quarters', is the headquarters of this district, being, apart from the dwelling-houses, a concentration of shops and stores, and comprising the village hospital, the Government School, the Post Office, the Warden Office, the Police Station — in short, all the public buildings of Mayaro.

Here, too, the people are up and stirring with the first beams of light from the coast. You can see that this is an agricultural area from the number of people 'dressed for the bush', with cutlasses and sacks, and with dogs trotting behind them. They would most likely be heading for their pieces of land in the bush somewhere along the Rio Claro Road. Depending on the time and the crop some are going to plant and others are going to reap, though with the favourite ground provisions like dasheen, tannia, and sweet cassava, any time would be time for planting and for reaping. These people, apart from growing ground provisions, are great growers of rice — though only for domestic use — and a dish of this home-grown 'creole' rice, cooked with coconut milk, and with the pigeon peas produced around the houses, is one of the typical Sunday meals in these parts.

In addition to those people who are going to work on their own lands, the labourers, most of them belonging to the Public Works Department, are already on the road, too. They consist of all types — forest-rangers, road-workers, drain-diggers. There are also the estate workers, and right away you would guess that this is also a cocoa-producing area, because of the number of estate people with long, knife-tipped bamboo rods, on their way to the cocoa plantations. For Mayaro is a centre of the cocoa industry. You encounter the labourers mainly on that thickly-forested road that leads to Rio Claro. By the time the sun is well up, all but the road-workers will have disappeared into the roadside forests.

In the clearing day, a lot of the womenfolk go down to Spring Flat for water. The children usually have to help their parents carry water before going to school, and you can see hosts of them at Spring Flat, with their buckets and pitch-oil tins. Spring Flat is on this very Rio Claro Road, just outside the village proper. From the village proper you go up a hill and descend steeply, and the thickly-forested road runs flatly for miles, and the first part of this 'flat' is called Spring Flat because there are springs here between the tall forest trees.

The women and children walk back to Quarters with the buckets and tins of water balancing on their heads on pads called 'cattas'. It is a pleasure to watch them, swaying gracefully with every step, their side-stretched hands helping to balance their bodies and rarely used to secure the tins on their heads. Their skill in doing this is almost unbelievable, but here no one takes notice, for it is no novelty.

As the children finish the chore of carrying water, there is another to be done — that of tying out the livestock to graze. Almost everyone here rears livestock; usually cattle, donkeys, pigs, and goats. The donkeys are becoming rarer and rarer as the days of donkey-carts are dying fast, but the cattle and goats are indispensable, for, apart from giving their meat, they provide the only fresh milk that the villagers drink. Pigs are about the commonest livestock around, and these animals, together with the chickens, and the kitchen garden of pigeon peas and bodi, sweet cassava and tomatoes, and the flower garden of zinnia, and the hibiscus hedge, add up to the typical yard.

After doing the morning chores of carrying water and tying out the livestock, the children prepare to go to school.

And now with the day bright and the time being nearly nine o'clock, the village is taken over by school-children. They come from Quarters itself, and the surrounding area, to attend the Government School on that hill by the Police Station called Station Hill. When it is nine o'clock and they are all inside the school, the village goes dead again.

By this time a lot will have been happening on the beach. The boatmen will have already seen schools of fish, and they will have already hurried back to the breakers, passing one end of the seine-rope to a swimmer of the shore group, and they will have already hurried back to sea, casting their nets, and encircling the fish. At this moment they will have been on shore again, and both groups — the boatmen and the shoremen — will have been pulling, as if for their lives, to bring the net with the catch ashore.

The net takes hours to haul ashore and the fishermen seem to be playing a game of patience with the sea, drawing in the rope inch by inch, pitting their weight against the resistance of the sea, their feet dug into the sand, gritting their teeth, grunting, their black torsos dripping with water and sweat.

They maintain the struggle, at moments crying out 'Hold!' and grimacing with the strain, when the sea tries to draw them forward, and then with bodies thrown against the rope and slanting almost to the sand, they make an all-out effort, and then they begin gaining ground again, slowly, doggedly, stumbling backwards, until the puller, up to his waist in water a short time ago, is down to his thighs now, then to his knees, then to his ankles, and then he is up on dry beach. He has gained all that from the sea! He glances at the amount of wet rope on the beach and as he goes into the water again, waist deep, in front of all his companions, there is renewed determination inside him. He pulls until his legs ache, and his guts feel like bursting; he throws all his strength into the effort, and inch by inch, heel by heel, he sees himself ease backwards, until, after what seems an interminable fight with the sea, the net, throbbing with fish, is sighted at the breakers. No wonder a cry goes up!

With the net in, people from the neighbourhood descend on the fish like vultures. They are impatient to buy, and soon there is confusion. For there is the living heap — which, apart from fish, may contain sea-crabs, jelly-fish, sea-weed, etc — and there are the fishermen, now suddenly important, the objects of attention, being implored, beseeched. And for this cherished moment the humble fisherman knows that he is king. He is still bathed in sweat, and his piece of short trousers is still dripping with sea-water. But he is the boss now and reacts accordingly. And now he is not above using abusive language as the housewives haggle. And the scene is chaos.

Nowadays, with Mayaro not so out-of-the-way as it used to be, this is a rare scene, for the fish merchants have already penetrated to this coast and they buy up whole catches for their supermarkets. With the result that these toilers of the sea have become a great deal more independent. Although their mode of fishing still recalls biblical times.

The holiday-maker, of whom little has been said, is a comparatively unobtrusive figure, save for the holiday month of August, when he and his friends and their families all but overrun the village. Normally, he is seen lying on the beach, bathing in the sea, or going for walks with his family underneath the palms. He is easily identifiable in his smart holiday wear and with his city talk. More often than not he is the medium- to higher-salaried city worker, and this holiday is a dream come true. For many years he has planned this holiday here for he has always heard of Mayaro. Now, from the time he gets up in the morning to the time he goes to bed at night it is one long session of bathing in the sea, lying on the beach, walking under the cool, shady palms, drinking coconut water, eating the meat of wild forest animals, which he has learned to call 'wild meat', and as he lies on the beach looking up into the void he is wondering how he will begin to tell about this when he gets back to Port of Spain.

All these holiday-makers are Trinidadians, for the foreign tourist hasn't yet discovered this part of Trinidad; he doesn't realise that it exists. This is true, not only of Mayaro, but also of the entire Eastern seaboard. Thus the Government has not yet thought of creating 'special attractions' for tourists here, and the East remains largely untouched and unspoilt.

Now, in mid-morning, things are rather quiet at Quarters, save for one housewife conversing with another over a hedge, or for another washing clothes in the sun and singing, or for the little movement from one shop to another in the centre of Quarters. Lolling about, also in the centre of Quarters, are the young boys who have left school and can't find work, some unemployed middle-aged men, and some old ones who have come out 'to see what is happening'. The shops have broad eaves, and under the eaves of every shop there is a market. Shaded from the burning sun the vendors under the shop-fronts sell fruits like mangoes, bananas, kymeats, cashews, governor plums, oranges, avocado pears, sapodillas, etc. and ground provisions like eddoes, tannia, dasheen, yam, and cassava, and even edible leaves like those of the dasheen plant, and spinach and packchoy. Sometimes when there is an excess of fish on the beach you can get fish here, too, and on occasions you can get wild-meat, and on Saturdays there is usually beef or pork on sale, thanks to someone who has slaughtered an animal to provide the village's Sunday meal, and a little 'change' for his pocket.

The morning passes calmly but the village's suddenly wakes to life again when the children burst out of school at twelve o'clock. It is lunch-time, and between now and one o'clock there is a great deal of activity and the children are everywhere. The shops are teeming with them, the cafés are cluttered with them, the Post Office is ringing with their voices asking whether there are any letters for them. Vehicles have to take special care in the streets now, and it is a good thing that the streets are very few — principally the Rio Claro Road, which runs due west from the beach; the Guayaguayare Road, which runs south from Quarters; and the Manzanilla Road, which runs north from in front of the Government School. At this time of day all sorts of carhorns blast the air. But after the school-bell sounds at one o'clock all goes dead again.

Afternoon in Mayaro is the quietest time of day. Very little happens — unless it is Saturday and there is something going on in the savannah. The savannah is right here at Quarters, beside the main Rio Claro Road, and there is usually something going on in it every Saturday. More often than not, a cricket match. This savannah, which is the grazing ground for cows and goats during the week, is the village arena on Saturdays, and sometimes on Sundays, when one of the 'fierce' cricket teams from Rio Claro, or Guayaguayare, or Manzanilla, comes here to do battle with Mayaro. And what looks like the whole village turns up to cheer Mayaro on and to harrass the 'invaders'. The pandemonium and the din shake Quarters. And if the match is close, or the other side is being 'tamed', the women are bound to scream and the men are bound to throw away their hats. And meanwhile, the young man who has to be trudging to the cocoa field at six o'clock the next morning is 'making style' out there in the middle with his willow and his Everton Weekes cap and looking as though he fell in milk.

In contrast, very little happens during a week-day afternoon, and the village is dead. Except that if you are at Quarters you might hear the mooing of a conch-shell and realise that the fishermen are calling people to buy fish. When the women hear the sound they hurry down to the beach for it means that fish is cheap. So many seines have brought in fish that the fishermen are almost giving the fish away to get rid of it. Because if they don't get rid of it by nightfall they will have to bury it on the beach. At times, and in season, fish is the commonest thing at Mayaro.

Now, in mid-afternoon, there are still boats in the sea, but many of the seine-men are dragging the nets in for the last time, and most of the boats are riding the breakers homewards. And soon the coconut trees begin to lengthen their shadows and the sun begins to 'cool'. The sight of children with school-books means that classes are already over for the day. Even the coconut-pickers are down from the trees and are 'slambaying' the picked coconuts — which is, gathering them into heaps, ready for the coconut crackers. Far away in the forests it is growing dark, and what with the wild cheeping of birds, and the racket of the parakeets overhead, the cocoa--pickers know that it is time to go home. The twilight meets the same faces on the road again, the same dogs, the same cocoa-rods. Only that the steps of the labourers are not as springy now as they had been when day was breaking.

At the seaside, the smoke billowing up from the houses underneath the palms is from the fire-sides preparing the evening meal. Everyone here calls the evening meal 'tea', but it is usually a chocolate drink and bakes. The boats are already under cover, but the lank, black figures are spreading out their nets to dry. Those who came in early are now piling up their dried nets in the sterns of the boats and thinking of the next day. The beach is deserted now. The pitch-oil lamps in the houses begin to appear and flicker, and among the palms fireflies flicker too. Every now and again one sees the blue-white flame of a gas-lamp in one of the beach-houses. Night hurries down. In the dusk, at Plaisance, just before the sea, comes a grunting sound and two dazzling headlights. It is the bus that is just arriving from one of its many trips to Rio Claro. Gloom shrouds the sea and the two headlands are already faint in the dusk. And if you have been at Mayaro a long time you yourself might say now: 'Hm! It's six o'clock already, oui.' For it is the end of another day.

Carnival

Andrew Carr

Trinidad's famous carnival takes place just before Lent, ending on the stroke of midnight as Ash Wednesday follows Mardi Gras. It owes its origin to the French. Although Trinidad was never French territory, the French settlers allowed in by the Spaniards towards the end of the eighteenth century soon outnumbered the Spaniards and dominated the island's culture. From 1783, for half a century, they developed the carnival: a season of gay and elegant festival extending from Christmas to Ash Wednesday. In addition to dinners, balls and *fêtes champêtres*, leading members of society, in disguise, would drive about the streets in their carriages, and in the evenings would visit the houses of their friends which were thrown open for the occasion.

The Africans began to take part in carnival after they had attained freedom under the Emancipation Bill of 1833. One of the things they brought to it was their portrayal of 'canboulay' (from the French *cannes brulées*, the burning-off of the cane on the sugar plantations, when they used to be mustered at the call of horns and conch shells, and marched off to put out the fires). At first canboulay was played on August 1, Emancipation Day, but subsequently it took place just after midnight on Dimanche Gras, the Sunday before the carnival. Thus the carnival on the streets underwent a transformation which jolted the gentry, who stopped participating in it although they kept up the disguise balls and the house-to-house visiting for *fêtes* entertained by small musical bands playing Spanish-type instruments: guitar, quatro, mandolin, tiplay and maracas or chac-chac. The coloured middle class threw itself with zest into such visiting while also, as time went by, participating more and more in the road mas' (mas' being short for masquerade) of the people.

This was played to the accompaniment of goat-skin drums and what one writer described as 'bands of music (*soi disant*) including those elegant instruments the tin kettle and salt box, the bangee and shack-shack'. The bangee appears to have been either the banja or the sanza, an African instrument consisting of a box with steel or bamboo tongues arranged to give different tonal effects. It was held in the palm of the hand and plucked with the thumb. The rhythmic tambour-bamboo percussion bands were to follow. Bamboo was cut to lengths of fifteen to eighteen inches for the higher notes and about three feet for the bass notes. The difference in size of bore gave different tonal effects. The smaller ones were struck together or with short lengths of wood, whilst the large ones were thumped on the ground. Later, the bottle and spoon was introduced. Bottles, particularly sonorous glass gin bottles filled to various levels with water and drummed with a spoon, added rich effects to this already engaging rhythmic ensemble. These were the precursors of the steelband, which originated in Trinidad about the year 1937.

As participation by the masses increased, there persisted for over sixty years a constant stream of upper-class criticism in the press about the low standard of the carnival. The festival used to be held on the three days preceding Ash Wednesday, but, after strong feelings were expressed about the desecration of the Sabbath, in 1843 it was restricted to the Monday and Tuesday. In the absence of any precise official statement as to time, the people began the festivities as early as possible, immediately after midnight on Sunday. The blowing of horns, more particularly conch shells, heralded the canboulay procession. A great crowd of people carrying lighted torches trooped through Port of Spain, a very dangerous custom in a town built chiefly of wood. By 1870, the canboulay was being decried as 'an unremitting uproar, yelling, drumming and blowing of horns', and the press claimed that carnival was becoming 'more thoroughly contemptible, and dying a natural death'. But the prophets of doom were to be proven wrong.

Carnival was, however, about to go through a crisis. In 1881 occurred the canboulay riots. An easy-going chief of police (described as a man of 'masterly inactivity') had been succeeded by the redoubtable Captain Baker, who sallied forth at the head of a posse in order to put an end to the canboulay with its dangerous torches and its riotous bands of nègres jardins (farm labourers) who specialised in stick-fighting. Rumour inflated his attempt to suppress the carnival's more disorderly aspects into an attempt to suppress carnival as a whole, and this infuriated the masqueraders. A fierce battle ensued between police and masqueraders.

This disaster had important consequences. On the instigation of the City Council, the Governor of the day, Sir Sanford Freeling, addressed the people at the Eastern Market on the following day, after having confined to barracks both the police and the military. To quote Andrew Pearse, he established 'a relationship based on mutual consent between the populace in its carnival formation and the authorities'. Freeling was censured by the Colonial Office, but his action was later upheld by a commissioner appointed to enquire into the riots. 'In my view,' said the commissioner, Mr. Hamilton, 'it is of great importance, more especially in a Crown Colony where the people are not represented in the Government, that they should be as it were taken into council on a matter of this sort, as by this means I fully believe they may often be got to acquiesce in a course which they would resent if it were forced on them.' It is agreeable to know that carnival's most violent incident ended in the triumph of commonsense and humanity.

An account of the Trinidad carnival would not be complete without some mention of what used to be called jamette carnival, which continued for many years after the riots. 'Jamette' derives from *diamètre*, and the designation implied 'beyond the diameter of respectability', or in other words, the underworld, which used to contribute to the occasion 'hordes of disreputable males and females ... organised into bands and societies for the maintenance of vagrancy, immorality and vice'. These were eventually brought under control by the police, and the canboulay processions ceased when six o'clock on the Monday morning became the official time for the carnival to begin. In the 1890s Ignatius Bodu, a city councillor and merchant of Marine Square (now Independence Square), affectionately known to the masqueraders as *Papa Bodi*, held the first competition for best disguised bands and individuals for the purpose of 'improving the moral tone of carnival', and that tone did indeed begin to improve. Moreover, other businessmen of Port of Spain, San Fernando, Arima and other centres of population became aware that this upward trend was good for business and worth encouraging.

The discontinuance of canboulay still left us with nègres jardins or stick-fighting bands, and although the police eventually forbade bands of more than ten men to carry sticks, they were to flourish in Port of Spain until well past the second decade of the present century. And these bands, with their stick-fighters or batonniers, continued to be found in towns and villages all over the country long after their counterparts in the city had ceased to exist. Up to the present time the art of stick-fighting, without its bloody ferocity, is still kept alive, mainly in rural areas where practice exhibitions and serious bouts under certain rules of restraint are held to the accompaniment of the stimulating calinda songs, a warlike type of calypso.

The very pleasurable old custom of house-to-house visiting in disguised bands diminished with the years, although a few people kept it up into the mid-1950s. Another aspect of pre-carnival activity which passed away with World War Two, was the nightly jump-up on the streets for about four weeks before carnival, with the exception of the Sundays. Police regulations forbade the wearing of masks, but they could be carried and put on when the celebrants reached a friend's house where a copious supply of rum and hot pelau awaited them.

Many years ago there used to be the custom of driving around the Savannah in decorated vehicles carrying on a mock battle with confetti and paper streamers, or serpentine rolls. It was a great deal of fun until thoughtless people began to mix pebbles and other harmful objects with the confetti, whereupon this pleasant diversion, and also that of throwing talcum powder, had to be abolished. In those days the streets on Ash Wednesday used to be an amazing sight and a telling reminder of the fun that had gone before.

In spite of inevitable changes over more than a century and a half, the pre-carnival season is still festive. New Year celebrations are no sooner over than the various calypso tents in Port of Spain, San Fernando and other areas begin to offer nightly entertainment. Five such places operated in Port of Spain in 1972. Four of them were led by famous carnival figures: the calypsonians the Mighty Sparrow (Slinger Francisco), known as the Calypso King of the World; Lord Kitchener (Aldwin Roberts), popular Road March King (the Road March being the calypso tune most frequently played on carnival days by the music bands); Lord Blakie (Carlton Joseph); and the Mighty Duke (Kelvin Pope), four times successively crowned Calypso King of Trinidad and Tobago, 1969—1971.

Club ole mas' begins about three weeks before the Carnival, when private clubs and other organisations hold disguise competitions for bands* of a comical nature, followed by dancing, or more properly, carnival jump-up. Almost all masqueraders wear masks for this kind of show, and portrayals are often based on some clever pun helped out by an explanatory placard, rather than on costume. They are frequently suggestive, and sometimes downright lewd.

Since the creation of the government-sponsored Carnival Development Committee in 1957, there has been a growing number of performances to enrich the seasonal enjoyment of carnival for about two weeks before the Monday and Tuesday festival days themselves. In brief, the CDC programme runs like this:

Calypso Fiesta: a performance by the twenty best calypsonians of the year — the cream of the crop, as we say — in competition for the selection of six or seven to compete against the reigning King at the Dimanche Gras show, for the honour of the year's crown, the Prime Minister's trophy and lucrative cash prizes.

Steelband Preliminaries: at the Savannah, usually on the second Sunday before carnival, fifty or more of the leading

* When one talks about a carnival band one means not just the music but the whole ensemble: the group, large or small, of people, who have banded together to interpret some particular theme — or just to jump-up together. Eds.

steelbands compete for the selection of fourteen of them to appear in semi-finals at the Friday night Panorama Show. Each plays a calypso tune on the move, before an audience of some forty thousand people. The show has to start at 10 o'clock in the morning to accommodate this lengthy programme. So physically exhausting has this been to everyone that efforts are being made to divide it into two or three shows.

Ole Mas' Competition and Preliminaries for Kings of Carnival:* in this, some forty kings in fabulous costumes compete for seven or eight selections to appear at Dimanche Gras finals. A competition for the witty and amusing club ole mas' bands is an additional feature of the entertainment.

Brassorama: a new feature introduced in 1972 embodying a competition for carnival instrumental bands together with other items of entertainment.

Folkorama: another new feature in 1972, projecting the best of the country's rich variety of folk presentations.

Panorama and Preliminaries for Queens of Carnival: here the fourteen semifinalists from the steelband preliminaries compete for the seven selections to appear at the finals on Dimanche Gras. Added to this immense musical treat are the preliminaries for the Queens of Carnival competition, which usually attract about forty contestants in gorgeous costumes.

Dimanche Gras: the grand Sunday night finale which incorporates the finals for Calypso King of the Year, and for King and Queen of Carnival respectively, and Best Panorama Steelband, with appropriate additional entertainment.

Other CDC Shows: the CDC also sponsors open-air steelband concerts throughout the country, and calypso shows mainly in rural areas. Two excellent shows with top-class calypsonians are given in Scarborough and Roxborough in Tobago each year. These programmes are conceived in the spirit of taking to the people annually the best in steelband and calypso talent.

* Each carnival disguise band has its king and its queen, whose costumes embody the band's chosen theme with the greatest possible splendour and elaboration. Those judged best are proclaimed Carnival King and Carnival Queen of the year. Eds.

Other pre-carnival attractions are the many competitions held for children, especially the one held by the Red Cross Society, which cater for several age groups from babes-in-arms to fifteen-year-olds.

The *Buy Local Carnival Jamboree* is an annual event since 1965, conceived and organized by The People's National Movement (the political party which has formed the government of the country since 1956). In collaboration with the Trinidad Manufacturers' Association, a competition for bands, couples, individuals, floats and calypsoes is presented, built around the theme of supporting local manufacturers.

It is usual for bandleaders to know in one year what they will present in the next. Sometimes they have made the decision even before the current carnival is over. Then, after several months of research and discussion of creative ideas with a close and small group of assistants and section-leaders, the big bandleaders will call in the artists to work on preliminary sketches of costumes. Some bandleaders with artistic talent do all the art-work themselves. Once the designs, colours, quantity and quality of material, and range of accessories and music have been approved and costed, the final art-work is undertaken. Several months before carnival, the day comes when the bandleaders put on a display of costume designs at their mas' camps, the headquarters of activities for the creation of the costumes. Each design is tagged with the price a participant would have to pay in order to wear it and play mas' with the band. These occasions are often gay affairs with music and an openhouse party given by the bandleader.

Visits to these displays are becoming an increasingly attractive pre-carnival activity for nationals and visitors alike, and so are visits to the panyards to listen to the practice sessions of the steelbands. Visitors from abroad sometimes make arrangements with bandleaders to come here to play mas' with the big colourful bands. Many Trinidadians resident abroad, especially in the United States and Canada, come down to participate in the carnival; and even when they cannot come, many of them provide an avenue of contact for overseas visitors wishing to participate actively in the festival.

Some enterprising bandleaders actually undertake trips to the US to purchase certain kinds of material unobtainable locally, and to make contact with people who want to join us in the fun. Over the last five years or more, it would seem to be a growing business, and such visitors seem delighted to share our enjoyment of the free spirit of carnival. I shall never forget the pleasant sight of a world-renowned North American lady anthropologist in angelic dress complete with wings and staff, experiencing carnival from the inside by chipping* along in Ken Morris's 400-strong band, Heralds Down the Ages.

How do people go about joining a carnival band, and how do the bandleaders cope with the organizational problems inherent in bringing out a band of perhaps eight or fourteen hundred men and women, or sometimes even more? The key to organization lies in decentralization. A few leaders try to organize the whole thing themselves, with the help of assistants, but it is far more common for the band to be divided into sections which consist usually of thirty or forty members, and sometimes of as many as a hundred. Each section has a leader who decides on the designs for the principal characters in his part of the band, and also for the floor members — the less important costumes which attend upon the central figures in the various sections. (For example, an elaborate costume representing the Moon might have a whole bevy of Stars as escort.) It is usual for the section leader to establish a sub-mas' camp. One band may have a score or more of them, all working towards the realization of the main bandleader's chosen theme.

A section leader proceeds to enlist his friends, who have often been in a band with him in previous years. They in turn introduce others, until the section reaches the predetermined number. The section leader takes care of the making of the costumes, particularly of that part of the job which involves the use of mass-produced material. A great deal of finishing is done by the players in their homes, but whatever can be ordered in bulk is the province of the leader

* 'To chip': to dance with the short, shuffling dance-step characteristic of jumping-up. Eds.

A costume for a leading figure in a carnival band — a simple one, as they go.

or leaders, to save energy and money. He also collects all monies due, with which to pay the music band — or bands, if the carnival band is a huge one — and so on, and he settles accounts with the bandleader.

In addition to headquarters, which may occupy two or three locations, some bandleaders establish country camps quite far from the city where forest and agricultural materials are gathered and processed for use in the production of costumes. All camps are hives of industry. They may be the home of the leader, or an empty building or group of buildings, or someone's garage, or the sheds in someone's backyard; and they will spill over all the available space on the premises.

Work goes on for several months. Some five or six weeks before the great event, full-time paid workers are engaged on a round-the-clock basis to meet the pressing demands of production. On whatever dates the carnival days may fall, there is always a frenzied last-minute rush: a stage at which visitors to the camps, year after year, express much admiration for the dedication of the teams of exhausted (though still cheerful) workers. A certain amount of panic, fatigue and chaos is surely an essential part of preparing for any great occasion. It is offset in the mas' camps by plenty of hot coffee and rum and by hot food served from time to time during the night. And apart from the camp activities, there are also the tens of thousands of people working on their costumes at home.

A considerable industry has developed round the carnival. It exercises the ingenuity of our leading artists, and the many aspects of costume-making demand a high standard of craftsmanship in metal-work (in which Ken Morris provides an outstanding example of the craftsman discovering the creative artist); in leather-work; in bead-work; and in wire-bending — the special art of making the intricate wire frames on which the more elaborate costumes are mounted. Imagination, ingenuity, discipline, leadership, organizing ability: carnival demands them all, and we meet the demand handsomely every year. It has been said that if we could channel half the thought, devotion and energy that we produce for carnival into economic production, Trinidad and Tobago would become one of the most productive countries in the world. In the meantime, our carnival bandleaders

Detail of a carnival costume. Nowadays many are exhibited when carnival is over, so that the work in them can be appreciated.

would do well to explore the possibilities of manufacturing costumes for Hollywood and other film-producing centres.

It is interesting to consider another aspect of the carnival: its psychological motivation. What, for example, makes some people play a particular type of masquerade every year for a life-time? An old friend of mine, Macdonald Tull, played mas' in the type of band called Devils and Demons for over sixty-six years. Beginning in 1903, at the age of fifteen, he graduated from small Imp portrayals to the magnificently robed Beelzebub, Satan and Lucifer. When he was eighty-one he assured me that come next carnival he intended to play again 'if God spare life'. Although such patriarchs do not come often, there are many old devotees in such traditional fields of masquerade as Devils and Demons, Clowns, Minstrels, Pierrot Grenade and Old Time Carnival. In 1971 Harold Thompson was the only surviving member of his original Minstrel band, Coons of Dixie, which originated in 1928. Comprising a few men and women with painted faces, they had sung in the tradition of the early Afro-American minstrels to the accompaniment of banjos and rattling bones.

And consider the sedate and distinguished educationist who is yearning to play the role of the chained Beast or Dragon in a Devils and Demons band; the leading surveyor who confesses to a burning desire to play a dirty little devil in skin-fitting tights known as a Jab-Jab, with a little wire tail behind him; or the young naval lieutenant who wanted so much to play Wild Indian that he got an old veteran to give him what he called 'Wild Indian lessons' in the lingo of this type of mas' so that he could speak of peace to other Wild Indians and avoid any combative situations. No doubt playing mas' offers many people a chance to express fantasies which are important to them.

Dr Errol Hill, in his book *The Trinidad Carnival — Mandate for a National Theatre*, says 'Nothing less than an explosion of theatrical talent fills the main streets of Trinidad and Tobago on the two days of carnival.' Moreover, he makes the point that 'for two days he (the masquerader) will be the living embodiment of his most fancied imagination.' Two further examples of this will serve to illustrate this aspect of carnival. Thousands will recall the entrance on stage at the

Queen's Park Savannah of Valmond Jones in the role of Nero in Harold Saldenha's famous band of 1955, Imperial Rome. Jones, a huge man, six feet two inches in height and weighing 260 pounds, wore a golden laurel wreath, a magnificent robe of royal purple and gold and a trailing cape some twenty-four feet long. In one hand he carried a harp and a weeping-cup. He approached his audience of thousands in majestic splendour, miming the demented Emperor perfectly. Wild-eyed he gazed upon them, and with a grand swish he twisted his great cape around him to uproarious acclaim from the stands. Not a word was spoken, but it was a memorable dramatic act. Again, take the case of Daniel Barker, another huge man, a stevedore on the Port-of-Spain docks who to this day loves to play characters of regal splendour. In 1964 he played the chief character in his band, Alaric, King of the Visigoths — who sacked Rome in 408 BC. It was a most impressive sight to see Barker in majestic progress on carnival days — he was a man conscious of the fact that he had sacked Rome and that he had the power of life and death over all whom he beheld. Today, in 1972, he still smiles with satisfaction over that portrayal which won for him the coveted title of Individual of the Year.

It must be very salutory to be able to shed some inhibitions and indulge in make-believe of one sort or another for a short while each year. A celebrated psychiatrist once said that because of its carnival Trinidad and Tobago ought to be one of the sanest countries in the world.

The Jour Ouvert — the dawn-of-day opening of the carnival — has changed a great deal with the passing years. At the beginning of this century and well into the 1930s it featured many individual performers apart from the bands. They took the form of Death; Pirates; Clowns; Red Indians purporting to be of the Orinoco region, and other imaginative varieties of Indian painted black, blue and even white; Jab-Jabs (devils); Robbers, blowing their whistles incessantly and threatening death and destruction as they importuned bystanders for pennies; the princely Pierrot, richly gowned and with tiny bells hanging from his garment, making speeches on great English kings and their military history, or on English literature, and sometimes delivering orations from

Shakespeare; his much less affluent counterpart, the Pierrot Grenade, in a gown of jute, giving forth his dissertations in French patois or Creole; Doctors and Tailors seeking fees; bewigged Judges and Lawyers and their clerks holding court at street corners; and Baby Dolls, women in frilly mini-dresses carrying large dolls, pretending to hold up errant putative fathers for 'money to mind the chile'.

Today, the Jour Ouvert begins at five o'clock on Monday morning, the time having been extended by an hour since 1963. Port-of-Spain's Independence Square is the focal point. Tens of thousands of spectators fill the streets and the pavements so that policemen on horseback are kept constantly on the move to preserve a passage-way for the steelbands and the masqueraders. In a short speech, the Mayor of Port of Spain, standing on the stage in front of the down-town grandstand, exhorts the people to maintain a clean and incident-free festival and wishes all — nationals and visitors alike — a happy and memorable carnival. A rocket fired off near the stage heralds the beginning of the carnival. An announcer begins to present to judges seated in the stand the various characters who have gathered on stage to compete for the title of King and Queen of Jour Ouvert, for which there are cash prizes and trophies. All are wearing masks. With the aid of explanatory placards, the individuals portray and sometimes lampoon celebrated personalities or notable events, local or international.

Faintly, in the distance, can be heard the deep throbbing sound of the bass booms and the metallic clanging of the approaching steelbands. As they converge on the square there is also the shiff-shiff of their followers' dancing feet. The characters on stage are soon swallowed up by the steelbands as they come in close succession. The revellers fill the street from side to side; they could not possibly be tighter packed as they dance past the stand to the strains of the music. This may be calypso, or it may be classical music arranged in calypso tempo (which the steelbands call their Bomb Tune for Carnival Monday). Jour Ouvert is not the occasion for spectacular costume. There will be some bands in colourful but inexpensive disguises, and a few huge bands comprising 1,000 to 1,200 men and women, but mainly this is the time of the festival devoted to the comic and the satirical; the grotesque; the double entendre and the ribald, and occasionally to the obscene. Transvestism is much in evidence.

People sit in the stands and watch Jour Ouvert, but essentially it is an occasion for participation rather than a 'show'. Many of the people following the bands will have come straight on from Dimanche Gras dances and fêtes, their heads already throbbing with rhythm and rum; and many others will now be swept into the current of celebration. It is they, rather than the spectators, who are embodying the spirit of carnival. It is an unforgettable experience to see this huge throng of all colours and racial strains, all ages, all classes, passing in their thousands unmindful of artificial barriers, with mundane cares thrown to the winds, yielding to the uninhibited pleasures of carnival.

Carnival Monday follows a distinct pattern. The uninhibited revelry of Jour Ouvert continues for five or six hours until ten or eleven o'clock in the morning. Everyone who can then goes home for a rest, and for refreshment which may consist of cooling home-made drinks such as mauby, sorrel or gingerbeer, or of sterner stuff like rum, gin or whisky with coconut water as a mixer, to soothe feelings of fatigue whilst maintaining the spirit of conviviality and hospitality so manifest everywhere at this time.

The colourful part of the carnival will begin about an hour after noon and will continue beyond dusk. Masqueraders change into lighter and lesser costumes for the night-time merriment in the clubs and on the streets. The night bands can be huge, often comprising 1,500 people or more. One must be ill or feeble to resist the big steelbands as they pass by, attracting everyone from grandparents to grandchildren to swell their enormous ranks. Such a road mas' steelband may have as many as 200 instruments mounted on trolleys, the trolleys being propelled forward as much by crowd-pressure as by the deliberate pushing of scores of helping hands. They are jostled and jolted, but never for one moment do the seemingly entranced players break the hypnotic pulse of the beat.

The grand extravaganza reaches its dizziest heights on the Tuesday — the Mardi Gras — when the costume bands that have made our carnival worldfamous parade in their full glory and wave after wave of brilliant colour, glitter and sound goes surging past the packed stands on the Savannah. Many of us have a weakness for the little 'home-made' bands which will be interspersed between the big ones; but it is the big ones which make the stunning effect. Often you can hardly believe you are watching human beings. Marvellous creatures — dragons, birds, gigantic flowers, castles, chariots, ships — go by in their endless variety, the only visibly human thing about them the little dancing feet just showing under the towering structure; and no sooner do you think that every possible combination of brilliant and daring colour must have been exhausted, than here comes a new one.

One of the great marvels, to the stranger, is how people can dance for hours in our tropical climate while wearing such elaborate and often heavy costumes. Perhaps you have to play mas' yourself before you can understand the power of the beat to keep people going. And we must admit, too, that rum plays its part: some masqueraders it knocks down, but many more of them it keeps jumping-up right through the day and evening until that strange moment at midnight when, with astonishing suddenness, everything stops. Mardi Gras is over. No more carnival till next year. It is not uncommon to see people who have been jumping-up for all they were worth until that very second, fall to the ground, dead to the world, as the music stops.

There are many trophies and cash prizes presented each year, and the eighty or ninety carnival bands which compete for them are placed in categories to facilitate judging. So are the six or seven hundred individual portrayals presented for adjudication. Today the main categories of band for competition are 'Ancient History', 'Modern History' and 'Original' — the last to accommodate the imagination and creativity of the modern bandleader who tends to be more artistic and inventive than his predecessors.

Then there are: 'Original-Topical' (portrayals of current events and the ways of life of different peoples); 'Original-Best-Dressed' (for those who want to play mas' in pretty costume without bothering about a theme); and 'Original-Humorous'. There are also a number of categories which sound somewhat freakish to the uninitiated but which have their specific meanings. 'Armed Forces' and 'Sailors on Shore-Leave' are perhaps self-explanatory (the latter allows for much fantasy, depending on the country the sailors are supposed to be visiting); but 'Fancy Sailors', 'Fancy Sea Bees' and 'Fancy Indians' may puzzle the visitor. In a band of 'Fancy Sailors' the traditional sailor costume has undergone an interesting evolution over the past fifty years. There was a phase of fuzzy cotton headpieces and large noses of curious shape, and this developed gradually into elaborate and beautiful headpieces made of papier-mâché, a really striking development of carnival art of which the bandleader Cito Velasquez is the great exponent; while the basic sailor costume, though still retained, is now so embellished as to be hardly recognizable. For some reason 'Fancy Sea Bees' (a category bequeathed to us by naval units associated with the American Naval Base at Chaguaramas during World War Two) have not yet developed artistic headgear, although their costumes are ornate.

The category 'Authentic Indians' covers attempts to portray the Indian peoples of North America (Harold Saldenha's Crees of Canada was an outstanding band of this type). 'Fancy Indians', on the other hand, are inspired by Sohtu American Indians — and sometimes by Africa as well. The word 'Fancy' in the carnival context means that imaginative freedom will be used in a theme's interpretation, although that freedom may develop and abidc by conventions of its own. When, on the other hand, authenticity is aimed for, a bandleader will take great pains over his research.

Then there are 'Warriors' and 'Clowns' (two categories which have deteriorated in recent years); 'Bats', both authentic and fancy; 'Minstrels'; 'Robbers'; 'Devils and Demons'; and the convenient heading 'Old Time Carnival' to cover an assortment of traditional disguises such as Pierrot Grenade, the princely Pierrot, Moko Jumbie, Burroquite and others.

Many people who know the Mardi Gras celebrations of other countries have said that Trinidad's carnival is the best in the world. What makes it the unique and attractive festival that it is? In my opinion, the most important element in its charm is that it is essentially a people's *fête*, with mass participation and a great deal of refreshing spontaneity about it in spite of the careful planning — planning by *the people*, not organized from without — which goes into it. Another factor is that it is allowed to flow freely where it wills. Some traffic control naturally has to be maintained, but it is kept to the minimum, and road mas' (the invasions of the streets by masqueraders) always wins over the benumbing effect of pageantry. Even the competition judging gives importance to the *free spirit* of Carnival, and that is how it should be. Then, although it hardly becomes a Trinidadian to say so, the imagination, originality and energy displayed in the organization of the bands does suggest that our people are exceptionally well endowed with artistry and ingenuity.

In some way peculiar to itself, carnival in Trinidad and Tobago is also a nation-building force. Year after year it brings together more and more of the diverse elements in our society to sing and dance and jump-up and fête together, and that can only contribute to a better mutual understanding among our people.

I fear that I have not managed to convey the full flavour of carnival; indeed, I know I have not, because descriptions always fail. You must experience it for yourself, and then you will probably react like a well-known English film producer of my acquaintance. It was only Monday evening — Mardi Gras was yet to come — when he started telling me that although he had read up on the subject he had still been totally unprepared for what he had seen. It was the most stunning, the most fabulous, the most magical, the most ... 'Hold it, Geoff,' I had to break in. 'You must leave at least *some* superlatives for tomorrow.'

The Calypso

Errol Hill

'We are word-containers. We are the memory of man. By the power of the word we give life to the king's actions for the benefit of the young. History contains no secret for us.' So runs a traditional chant of the *griot* among the Mandingo people, once the most powerful empire in West Africa. Six hundred years ago *griots* of this African nation held an esteemed place among the nobility. They were the repositories of their country's history, of its music, dances and poetry. They were the antecedents of the Trinidad calypsonian.

At one of the numerous traditional festivals in Nigeria today, the whole community turns out to judge an annual song contest between rival masqueraders. The masked balladeers sing original compositions about past and current events as dancers gyrate around them and throngs of supporters echo their choruses. The winner is acknowledged to be songster of the year. The *ekwechi* festival may combine ancient fertility rites with ancestor worship, but in externals it is no different from the annual calypso king competition in Trinidad and Tobago.

The African heritage of the calypso is clearly established. Praise-songs and songs of derision by professional minstrels and community choirs abound among West African peoples, ancestors of New World black men. The reliance on choral refrain, the dancing chorus, the call-and-response structure, all provide striking parallels in form between the calypso and indigenous songs of the old Guinea coast. Even the name, 'calypso', (or, more correctly, 'kaiso') has been traced to a West African source.

Yet African heritage alone cannot account for the popularity of the calypso, or for its longevity and the vigour of the form's growth. Now accepted as the national song of Trinidad and Tobago, in years past the calypso had to fight for survival and later for the recognition long denied it. Currently the output of calypsoes is staggering. In 1970, during the carnival season that is from Christmas to Ash Wednesday over one hundred and fifty calypsonians entered the lists to compete for the calypso king's crown. As a rule singers do not revive old calypsoes during the season unless by special request of the audience. As each calypsonian composes a minimum of three new compositions every year (and many singers produce over that number), the crop of new calypsoes annually surpasses five hundred.

Universal acceptance of the calypso attests to its catholicity of form. Its melodic and verbal structure incorporates the major types of traditional song functionally associated with the people of Trinidad and Tobago. Examples of these are the digging songs chanted by people at work; belair and calinda songs when they play; shango and shouter baptist revival songs when they worship; and insurrectionary songs such as were sung by the slaves in revolt.

Atilla the Hun (Raymond Quevedo) considers that the earliest surviving calypso was a rebellious song of the slave period in which the blacks expressed their determination to worship the god of their choice despite the orders of the planters against pagan ceremonies:

LEADER: *Ja Ja Romy oh!*
CHORUS: *Ja Ja Romy Shango.* (repeat first two lines)
LEADER: *Ja Ja Romy oh meti beni.*
CHORUS: *Ja Ja Romy Shango.*

Shango, the Yoruba god of thunder, lightning and iron, is a good master and his worship must be observed. Atilla was the first calypso historian. As professional calypsonian, city councillor, deputy mayor, and member of the country's parliament, he was chiefly responsible for winning recognition of the calypso as a valid art form indigenous to the people of Trinidad and Tobago.

Musically, the calypso embraces melodic characteristics from the diverse nationalities that comprise the mixed population of the nation. African rhythm predominates, but calypso melodies have been strongly influenced by Spanish music through nearby Venezuela. In the first decades of this century many calypsoes were musically identified by the term *paseo*, a popular Venezuelan dance. Music of French, Irish and English origin has been adopted into the calypso repertoire. In more modern times oriental-flavoured music from Indian and Chinese elements of the population has filtered in. Thus the calypso appeal has widened to include ethnic groups whose indigenous cultures, remaining fairly intact on transplant to the Caribbean, have been less susceptible to integration into the national culture.

Oral tradition has it that the first known Trinidad calypsonian or 'shantwell' (Fr: *chanterelle*) was Gros Jean, a professional singer attached to the retinue of Pierre Begorrat, one of the early French immigrants to the island who arrived from Martinique in 1784. Testimony from old veterans of the nineteenth century carnival tents, however, affirms that the 'cariso' was a woman's song and dance, usually performed in stick-fighting yards as an interlude between bouts of the more manly art of duelling with hardwood sticks. Both traditions are probably correct.

What is certain is that from an early date the annual carnival festivities provided the main stimulus for the composition and public rendition of these traditional songs. In 1838, for instance, the year in which slave apprenticeship ended, the local press spoke of 'disgusting and indecent scenes' enacted in the streets at carnival time, one scene being 'the African custom of carrying a stuffed figure of a woman on a pole, which was followed by hundreds of Negroes yelling out a savage Guinea song'. This could actually be the first road-march calypso chanted by revellers as they paraded the streets in masquerade. It was apparently in an African tongue, or at least was thought by the writer to be of African origin. However, as the century progressed, the majority of carnival songs were composed extemporaneously in patois or the French Creole language which was the common medium of intercourse among the populace.

In 1851 we have another reference to a characteristic of the carnival songs, their personal ribaldry. A correspondent writing in a Trinidad paper reported that a certain individual, whom he accused of immoral conduct, was personified and derided by revellers during the masquerade 'whilst the names of his victims are being sullied in the streets, and made the subject of the ribald songs and jests of the people'. The masquerade calypsoes did not indulge in mudslinging simply for the fun of it. The songs were addressed primarily to an unlettered working-class audience. They served as newspaper and tabloid to convey information, offer commentary, and disseminate juicy gossip about the affairs of individuals belonging to all strata of society.

Nineteenth-century society in colonial Trinidad was indeed arbitrarily stratified. At the base were the numerically superior black ex-slaves who were still denied many of the privileges of free people. No better off were the thousands of Asiatic Indians indentured to the plantations as replacement for slave labour. They were mostly confined to their barrack-room hovels on estates. The free coloureds thought of themselves as better off than the ex-slaves but were just not accepted among the largely European ruling class. This upper crust was divided by national origin: early Spanish colonizers, French settlers, and British administrators; and cross-divided too by political adherence to either republican or royalist beliefs. They vied with each other to preserve or assert their power and privilege, but they were united in denying any extension of that privilege to the masses beneath them. The one great leveller was the calypsonian. He sang with courage and wit, debunking the great and defending the small. His was a salutary function in a society composed of explosive elements. His freedom to speak out with impunity was hard-won and must at all costs be preserved.

At the carnival of 1881 the famed canboulay riot took place. One report has it that Captain Baker, Inspector of Police, had made a bet with a fellow club-member that he could suppress the stick-fighting bands which roamed the early morning carnival streets. These bands had grown out of a ritual celebration of slave emancipation. The adherents had developed stick-fighting into a highly skilled art. At carnival time they paraded the streets seeking a test of skill and valour, and to pay off old scores. They sang calinda songs accompanied by drums. Previous unsuccessful attempts had been made to crush the bands and now the redoubtable Captain intended to assert his authority. Supported by a party of picked policemen he mounted his horse and rode to battle.

The encounter took place in the eastern section of the city. The police were routed and later besieged in their barracks. Before the day was over victorious masqueraders were chanting songs of derision at them and an effigy of Baker was buried at a mock funeral by the revellers. In an attempt to justify the Captain's actions, the official report of the riot referred to 'the practice of singing the vilest songs, in which the names of ladies of the island are introduced' on the carnival streets. Thereafter, to the end of the century, there were many newspaper protests against indecent and obscene songs, in patois, sung publicly at the annual masquerade.

Calypsoes in English appeared two years before the century closed. In his composition, 'What is Calypso', Lord Executor (Philip Garcia) gives credit to Richard the Lion Heart (Norman LeBlanc) for introducing the first full English calypso. Executor, master of Me Minor calypsoes and of extemporaneous singing, made his first calypso in 1900, so he speaks with authority. LeBlanc's English composition was a political volley levelled at the Governor, Sir Hubert Jerningham, who in 1898 threatened to abolish the Port of Spain City Council. The chorus ran:

Jerningham the Governor,
Is a fastness in-to you,
Is a rudeness in-to you,
To break up the laws of Borough Council.

The turn of the century was in fact an important period of change for the calypso. It was a long-standing practice in the weeks preceding carnival for masquerade bands to assemble at night in backyard tents and rehearse their calypso choruses. These gatherings were frowned on by the authorities (the drum had been abolished after the canboulay riot) and despised by respectable people in the town. Now at last people of influence began to attend the tent practices to get a foretaste of the new songs and to enjoy an evening of native wit and spicy humour. That calypsonians were now using English lyrics was largely responsible for the new attitude towards them. Lyrics were printed in full in the daily press and, for the first time, the name 'calypso' was seen in print to designate the carnival song.

By the end of the World War One, carnival tents were charging a small admission fee for patrons who wished to hear the calypsoes in advance of their rendition on carnival day. Programmes were arranged with greater care; rival singers were invited to visit and pit their skill at versifying with the home-based songster. Young dancing girls were introduced to enliven the evening's entertainment. It would not be long before the extemporaneous form of the calypso gave way to prepared and well-rehearsed lyrics, and the calypsonian separated himself from the responsibilities of managing a carnival band to become a full-time professional singer.

The man credited with turning the calypso tent into a thriving entertainment business is Chieftain Douglas, a ticket collector on the government railway. The tent which he opened in 1921 was bigger, cleaner, brighter and more comfortable than any other. It seated three hundred patrons. It was covered with railway tarpaulins to keep out the rain. It was well lighted by gas lamps in place of the old kerosene flambeaux which smoked and sputtered. And it had a stage for the performers. Douglas gave three performances a week, entertaining the audience with up to two hours of calypsoes which, to begin with, he alone sang, supported by a chorus from his masquerade band, the Railway Millionaires. It was doubtless a strain and partly explains why many of his calypsoes were of the ballad variety and ran to well over a dozen verses. Once established, he brought in guest singers from neighbouring tents and in return he would visit other tents to perform when his was dark. He was among the last batch of calypsonians to lead a masquerade band on the road.

The nineteen thirties launched the calypso on the international market. Every year leading singers were sent to New York to record their most popular numbers for sale at home and to meet a growing overseas demand. Calypsonians, facing foreign audiences and meeting the demands of professional recording studios, improved their technique, broadened their content, and refined individual singing styles. America's entry in the war against Hitler further internationalized the calypso as GIs posted overseas took the songs with them. In the well-publicized case involving the pirating of Lord Invader's (Rupert Grant) 'Rum and Coca-cola' calypso by a top-rated American singing trio, it was disclosed that five million discs of this song had been sold all over the world.

Back home increasing professionalism imposed heavier overhead costs and higher wage bills on tent managers. They sought programme novelties to attract more patrons. From these innovations arose the duet and drama in calypso. The duet did not last. After a few years the experiment of two singers taking alternate verses in a single composition was dropped except for the teaming up of Lord and Lady Iere (Randolph Thomas and Edna Pierre) whose 'Ice Cream Block' calypso remains a minor classic. But the calypso drama, which developed from the duet, persisted. Today it is a normal expectation that at least one drama will be presented each season as an appropriate climax to a calypso tent programme.

To call these miniature operettas 'drama' is, perhaps, to dignify them. They are little more than twelve- to fifteen-minute skits in which the dialogue is mostly sung in rhymed calypso couplets or alternate rhyming lines. Much comic mime is introduced. The orchestra plays throughout, accompanying sung and spoken dialogue, underscoring comic business, and providing a musical bridge between short dramatic sequences. Here the work of the band leader is of central importance because, although the singer composing the drama will have a melody for it, the orchestra leader orchestrates and arranges the music, adding considerably to the overall success of the presentation. Prior rehearsal by the actor-singers is cursory; a distinct impression of spontaneous, even improvised action is conveyed at each performance. Despite its abbreviated scope and casual preparation, the calypso drama represents one form of truly indigenous theatre and might yet prove to be an important contribution to the growth of a national drama.

What makes a great calypso? Few of the five hundred songs composed each year will survive. Some will. Many great calypsoes of days gone by are quickly brought to mind in discussion with calypso devotees today. The following calinda chorus from the days of stick-fighting bands is partly in patois and must date back sixty or more years. It is still affectionately recalled and chanted today:

O Lawd! de glorious morning come,
En bataille-la!
Depuis mama fait mwen,
Nom paka ba mwen bois
En bataille-la!
(O Lord! the glorious morning come
For the stick-fight!
Since my mother gave birth to me,
No man has ever beaten me
In the stick-fight!)

Another chorus, this time a famous road-march, recalls the spontaneous public jubilation that erupted when news broke that World War One had ended:

Argos paper, latest telegram! (repeat)
Germans surrender
Under the British commander!

The fact that the *Argos* was the champion of the working classes in their fight to have the carnival reinstated as a people's festival after the wartime interregnum gave added piquancy to the victory parade. Officialdom took note and revived the carnival.

Many memorable war calypsoes can be cited but none will ever surpass one by the Growling Tiger (Neville Marcano) about the unprovoked attack on Ethiopia by Mussolini's fascist troops. With a majestic musical score that has a grandeur all its own, Tiger sang passionately:

Africa, India, China, Europe — all have contributed beauty to Trinidad and Tobago.

The gold, the gold,
The gold, the gold,
The gold in Africa
Mussolini want from the Emperor.

Abyssinia appealed to the League for peace,
Mussolini actions were like a beast,
A villain, a thief, a highway robber,
And a shameless dog for a dictator.

So the first quality of a great calypso is that it should be both timely and timeless. It must be effective in the first season of its rendition but it should retain a power to move us years after the event it describes has receded from our concern.

Next, the great calypso must cohere in all its parts. Content, treatment, music, verbal facility, should combine as if they belonged together inextricably. One looks for wit and humour, of course, but also for colourful language, for metaphor, for a melodic and rhythmic structure that strengthens the impact of the performed calypso and is in no way inharmonious with the idea or story. The following verses from one of the most appealing calypsoes of all time is by Atilla. It records the first visit of a dirigible airship to Trinidad in 1933:

One Sunday morning I chanced to hear
A rumbling and a tumbling in the atmosphere.
(repeat first two lines)

I ran to stare, people were flocking everywhere,
Gesticulating and gazing and pointing in the air.
It was the Graf Zeppelin which had
Come to pay a visit to Trinidad.

I gazed and the knowledge came back to me,
How wonderful the work of man can be.
To see that huge object in the air
Maintaining perfect equilibrium in the atmosphere,
Wonderfully, beautifully, gloriously,
Decidedly defying all the laws of gravity.
It was the Graf Zeppelin which had
Come to pay a visit to Trinidad.

Top: Arrowing sugar-cane, Trinidad's most important crop.
Bottom: The Savannah, Port of Spain, with racehorses at their early morning exercise.

Every great calypsonian infuses a song with his own inimitable personality, giving each of his compositions its definitive rendition which thereafter adheres to it. Calypsonians develop singing styles peculiar to their talents and this individuality of performance leads to great rivalry, not so much among the singers themselves as among their supporters. It is unheard of for the followers of one calypsonian to be converted to the merits of a rival singer's style. Songsters reputed for innovative styles of performance include the Roaring Lion (Hubert Raphael DeLeon), the Mighty Spoiler (Theophilus Phillip), and the Lord Melody (Fitzroy Alexander) to name but a few. Lion is known for fleetness of expression and a strong rhythmic flow. Spoiler was a phlegmatic singer as he drawled out the most fantastic concoctions of humour ever heard in a calypso tent. Melody is a pantomimist. His calypsoes are action songs which he attacks with gusto and verbal bravado.

Entertainment value ranks high in judging the great calypso, but its worth must also depend partly on moral insight and observation, on the ability of the composer to aim, however obliquely, at understanding or improving the human condition. Most people would be surprised at the notion that calypsoes have a moral quality. Yet a great many do when they are genuinely conceived rather than the product of some rhymester alien to the milieu who composes salacious ditties for the pop record market. 'Death is Compulsory' by Lord Kitchener (Aldwin Roberts) is an all-time classic among thought-provoking calypsoes, as are 'The Human Race' by Lord Pretender (Alric Farrell), 'Federation' by the Mighty Sparrow (Slinger Francisco) and, most recently, the timely 'Black is Beautiful' by the Mighty Duke (Kelvin Pope). These are random selections from a host of calypsoes that deserve a place in the calypso hall of fame when that long overdue building is at last established in the country where calypso was born.

'We are word-containers. We are the memory of man.' The calypso repertoire is as wide and varied as it is long. Patriotic songs, philosophic songs, songs in praise of human achievement or in dismay at human degradation, songs of protest and songs of celebration, fantasy, satire, love, the battle of the sexes, songs of crime and tragedy, of racial prejudice and pride, the whole spectrum of human experience is to be found in the calypso. It is at once a social document of the country's history, a compendium of the people's language, an archive of their music. It is an accurate indicator of the people's pulse on matters of national concern.

The calypsonian serves his country equally as well as the *griot* of ancient Mali served his. But our native bard has not received the place of honour he deserves. Perhaps it is just as well. No honour or patronage should impede his freedom to speak out. In the nineteen thirties government censorship of the calypso was strongly advocated. It was a time of social and political unrest; the workers' leader, T. Uriah Butler, had been arrested and jailed. This was the moment that King Radio (Norman Span) chose to release one of his defiant calypsoes:

They want to licence my mouth,
They don't want me to talk,
Ai-ai, I ain't Butler.
They want to licence my foot,
They don't want me to walk,
Ai-ai, I ain't Butler.
But if is blood, sweat and misery,
We mean to fight till we get our liberty.

Radio's uncompromising spirit must be protected. His freedom to speak out against the excesses of his day is our guarantee of freedom in our own time.

Sparrow as Poet

Gordon Rohlehr

Trinidad's calypsonians are frequently called its folk-poets, though those who describe them thus seldom explain what they mean by the term. One of the major difficulties in discussing the work of Sparrow or of any other calypsonian as poetry is that the calypsonian combines the arts of musician, singer, raconteur, dramatist, showman and dancer. It is always a futile exercise to discuss the language of the calypso as something divorced from the music, rhythm, and the audience for which the calypso is intended; for calypso is part of an oral tradition and its full meaning only comes across in the act of performance.

Sparrow has added a sense of true professionalism to the world of the calypso. He has blended the art of the raconteur with that of the showman, and in his performance, as in his lyrics, he places a new emphasis on the body. Whereas Spoiler and calypsonians of his era placed more emphasis on facial expression and comic gestures, Sparrow emphasises movement, the synchronization of words, rhythm and dance. In Spoiler, as in Cypher, metre exists as a frail skeleton over which the words are stretched, or rather scattered, but which they threaten continually to defeat. In Sparrow, metre exists as a powerful force which the singer cannot afford to ignore, but which he needs to conquer and against which he must establish such strong rhythmic patterns as the sense of what he is saying demands. Sparrow seems to be continually at war against the confining strictures of the basic beat. It is this which has made his contribution to the rhythm of calypso no less than revolutionary. One thinks of calypsoes like 'Sir Garfield Sobers', 'Shanty Town

People', 'Carnival in 68', 'The Governor's Ball', or earlier efforts such as 'Robbery with V', 'Wahbeen and Grog', 'Ten to One', 'Renegades', and a host of others.

It is too little recognized how Sparrow in life, as well as in art, blends the traditional with the new, straddles two generations as well as two strata in society, and strives to preserve some sense of continuity in an age when the senior and junior generations can scarcely recognize each other as belonging to the same society. The continuity with the past which Sparrow has preserved has had its negative as well as its positive side. For example, Sparrow carried over from the 1940s into the 1950s the 'Saga Boy' attitudes of violence, easy living off immoral earnings, defiance towards the world in general and especially towards rival Saga Boys; masculinity, sexual superiority, dream-fantasy, flamboyance in dress and manner, elaborate masking and self-evasion, and even a certain sadism. His calypsoes, early and late, have been full of these themes; real change in his work has been in manner rather than in matter.

Indeed, 'Jean and Dinah', the calypso which first won Sparrow the crown, was really a fresh treatment of a worn-out theme. The Yankees had left Trinidad ten years before, and Kitchener, in 'Ding Dong Dell', Growler in 'Female Taxi-Driver', and even Spoiler in 'Marabella Pork-Vendor' (1947) had already commented on the dire effects of their departure on the local skin-trade. The Saga Boys, whose mouthpiece the calypsonians usually were, had been wounded to the quick by the presence of the richer and more socially acceptable American soldiers. Kitchener's 'My Wife Left Me For A Yankee' is a confession of the impotence and futility which the Saga Boys had been made to endure during the occupation. In the generation before the Yankees, the Saga Boys used to boast that they could hire out the bodies of their womenfolk and still preserve their hearts. The Yankee presence revealed the economic basis of the Saga Boy-Jamette relationship, the essential sterility of the Saga Boy pose, and the latent inferiority complex of the entire class of jobless, desperate young men, who masked their psychic castration by a cynical pose and a celebration of irresponsibility.

Calypsoes like 'Ding Dong Dell' and several others in that genre, were really bitter songs of revenge, mocking the plight of the broken good-time girls. Sparrow's 'Jean and Dinah' was of this school; as indeed, were a number of his early efforts, all of which laughed at the hardship facing the destitute prostitute. Why were they so successful? Part of the explanation must have been that the pride of the West Indian male had been so severely hurt that he was still preoccupied with the idea of making his woman suffer. This, however, was not the whole story. In those days before the Chaguaramas issue and the government-sponsored anti-Yankee feeling of the late fifties, what would have attracted the crowd to 'Jean and Dinah', was the freshness and aggressiveness of rhythm, the new bounce, the sureness of tone of voice, the vitality and biting cynicism with which Sparrow was able to invest a worn-out theme ...

It's the glamour boys again
We are going to rule Port of Spain
No more Yankees to spoil the fête
Dorothy have to take what she get
All of them who used to make style
Taking their two shillings with a smile
No more hotel and Simmonds bed
By the sweat of thy brow shalt thou eat bread.

One notices that as yet Sparrow's lyrical line is short, punchy, uncluttered by syllables, and contains the type of clarity and force at which Kitchener and Melody were especially expert. It is the last line that indicates a little of the difference between his style even then, and that of the generation before. Much less rhetorical than Lion was, and is, much less given to the use of long words which Atilla transmitted into the 1940s from the improvised 'picong' calypsoes of the late 1920s and thirties, and with a better sense of timing than both of these 'Golden Age' figures, Sparrow was able to inject a new economy and terseness into his lyrics. In typical folk style, he ends the narrative with an aphorism that summarizes the entire issue — 'By the sweat of thy brow shalt thou eat bread.' It is Jehovah handing down the law again to an erring humanity whose independence he can never tolerate. It is the authoritarian West Indian male seeking revenge on his semi-emancipated woman. It is also Sparrow, the new symbol of the transcendent individualism, will-to-power and will-to-self, which were to imbue the political and social striving of pre-independent Trinidad.

But perhaps, the most important feature of that last line is the 'artistic' one. The aphorism from Genesis is wrenched out of its serious religious context, and made to serve the purpose of irony which celebrates amorality rather than moral instruction. The tendency to place irony above simple moralizing has been one of the major features of Sparrow's poetic art. Its early and consistent appearance in his work has separated him in consciousness from most other calypsonians of the 1955—1966 decade, which he has indisputedly ruled with rigour, at times with violent self-assertion, and with an inability to endure defeat. The decade before Sparrow had produced the legendary Spoiler, a genius of the absurd with the wryest irony and the most fascinating wit possible. His peculiar contribution to the calypso form had been to explore the hilarious borderlands between apparent sense and apparent nonsense, and also to express the dry laughter of a bizarre age, on the edge of hope, but too familiar with failure and stagnation, and too directionless to make much effort for change.

Sparrow belongs to a different age, and although he has preserved many of the attitudes of the earlier generation, is as much the product of the traumatic beginning of a new era. His boyhood was spent at a time when the possibility of an emerging local leadership seemed about to be realized. In 1956 he was twenty-one, his coming of age coinciding with the birth of the PNM, the acquisition of what was termed 'full internal self-government', and the slender possibilty of nationhood. The nationalist surge of the late fifties, enhanced by the Chaguaramas issue, imbued the entire society with a sense of its hitherto unrealized potential, and allowed a mind like Sparrow's breathing-space and purpose for the kind of poise and balance necessary for a social comedy, uninhibited by either rancour or narrow moralizing.

Atilla, master of the decade of the late thirties to the late forties, belonged to an age of unremitting protest against the dying Crown Colony regime. His political ambition was the complement of Spoiler's sense of the absurd. He has often been termed a satirist, but in reality he had little time for irony. His political calypsoes, like Executor's of a generation before, were more in the nature of simple complaint, in which the calypsonian stated what he thought was wrong, and how it could be set right. Sparrow, who has sung a number of calypsoes of this type (e.g. 'The Base', 'William the Conqueror', 'The Present Government', (1961), and even the famous 'Pay as you earn' and 'No Doctor No'), is largely responsible for the development from complaint to what is at times a most complex satire.

With 'Yankees Back Again', the less famous sequel to 'Jean and Dinah', one sees the first real sign of Sparrow's capability in this new direction. There Sparrow notes that the Yankees who had just purchased the oil refineries at Point-à-Pierre (about 1958) were returning not as transient soldiers, but as rooted capitalists, whose aim it is to buy out the whole of Trinidad, and then to take Tobago as dessert. He shows a keen awareness of the meaning of what is now termed 'neo-colonialism'; and this was before Independence.

Well, the days of slavery back again
Ah hope it ain't reach in Port of Spain
Since the Yankees come back over here
They buy out the whole of Point-à-Pierre
Money start to pass, people start to bawl
Point-à-Pierre sell the workmen and all.

Then the chorus recreates the atmosphere of the auction block, to show that we are still in the days of slavery:

Fifty cents a head for Grenadian
A dollar for born Trinidadian

Tobagians free, whether big or small
But they don't want no Bajans at all.*

The second stanza describes the spread of the American interests in the islands, and hints at the impossibility of any real independence.

Well, it looks as if they going mad
To sell the refinery in Trinidad
Ah hear they tackling the Pitch Lake
But ah keeping cool for Heaven's sake
Next time they will buy Ste Madeleine cane
Then it's easy to capture Port of Spain
But when they buy Trinidad and you think they stop
They taking Tobago for lagniappe.

The spreading blight of the Yankee dollar is described almost in terms of a military campaign. The vision is not only comic, but precise and prophetic, with wider implications than Sparrow guessed. Here in jest, and probably by accident, one has the age-old connection between imperialist commerce and imperialist militarism identified. 'Capture' in the stanza above is a word brilliantly chosen. Port of Spain, the capital city, itself not comparable with industrial centres is, however, the calypsonian's Mecca, the world in which he is really king, and whose 'capture' by foreigners is for him ultimate humiliation.

The last stanza tells why this is so. The new invasion could mean a fresh humiliation for the 'glamour boys', who have just re-established a shaky rule over the local girls, and now face a subtler challenge. This time, the calypsonian says, the Yankees are no longer the he-man soldier-type in quest of flesh, but executives, and, he hints, sexually sterile types, in quest of a labour market to exploit:

But now, it's entirely different
The Yankees don't want entertainment.
The way they pack up in Point-à-Pierre
They entertaining one another down there.

* Barbadians have been traditionally the enemy, since the late nineteenth century when they were employed in the Trinidad Police Force: hence Sparrow's lofty denial of value to them, even on the 'auction block'.

So any woman who want Yankee money
Turn Grenadian and work like a donkey.

An important calypso, it passed without commentary — Sparrow had been in singing business for little more than two years. The poise and mockery of this calypso, which were echoed in an entirely different kind such as 'Monica Dou Dou', reached their ultimate refinement in 'Police Get More Pay' (1959—1960). Here Sparrow is able to comment that the police pay rise instituted by Mr Ulric Lee, a member of the first PNM* Government, led to untold misery in the police force, since the public was now unprepared to pay policemen the usual hush-money or bribes.

Them policeman mad, mad, mad,
Ah say they wild here in Trinidad
The Government raise on they salary
Still they unhappy.
With this raise people know they get
They don't want to pay they debts.

It is the chorus that is truly brilliant and poetic. The process of accepting bribery is effectively captured in the rapid scurry of syllables which are almost whispered, in the first line of the chorus. The words trip off the tongue — 'They used to get a shilling here, collect a shilling there' — The listener can almost see the long arms and the swift fingers of the law accepting and rapidly pocketing bribes, here, there and everywhere. Here is the entire chorus:

They used to get a shilling here, collect a shilling there,
Now all o' that stop.
And if they only say they broke, people say they making joke,
'Ah hear you pay gone up'.
Now the whole force in misery
No more loans and credit you see.
I hear they planning to lock up Lee
For raising they salary...

* People's National Movement, founded in 1956, the ruling party since that date to the present time.

The parliamentarian becomes unpopular because in reforming the low salary-scale for policemen, he has, unfortunately, encouraged a sense of morality in the public to which the police are unaccustomed. It totally upsets the equilibrium, by undermining a long-established and time-tested system of bribery which was really a not inconsiderable source of the policemen's income under the starvation wages of Crown Colony Government. But the matter doesn't end there. Comic richness achieves its highest point with the last four lines of the final stanza:

Mr Lee Oh! Oh! Mr Lee,
You better drive carefully
Every traffic policeman got you on he mind
And ah hear Johnson raise the fine!

A joke always loses its effect when explained, but this one merits some analysis. Johnson is the magistrate, and, like the policemen, on the side of the law. He has raised the fine for traffic offences, most probably to subsidize the same pay rise that Mr Lee has given the policemen. But Lee's piece of legislation has defeated its end by creating a new misery for the people it was meant to help. The police will therefore apprehend Mr Lee at the first opportunity and haul him up before Johnson, whose raised traffic fines will at least ensure that Mr Lee shares in some of the misery that he has helped to create. But since Mr Lee in paying Johnson's fine will be subsidizing his own pay increase to policemen, he will, by the logic of the calypso, be causing them further misery and confusion. They will therefore have to arrest Mr Lee again.

If one accepts the original premise of the calypso that a policeman is naturally attuned to a system of bribery, then all this is implied, and the listener is caught in an eternal circle of absurdity. I don't think that I can creating subtleties where they don't exist. There was precedent for this calypso in the Spoiler tradition, and, as we shall see, Sparrow himself achieves a similar ironic complexity time and time again. One of Spoiler's most famous calypsoes, 'Himself Told Himself', concerns similar confusion among officialdom. A magistrate is charged for speeding while on his way to Court. But since he is the only magistrate in the district, he is forced to try himself. He is therefore both accused and accuser, and also the judge whose opinion will resolve the affair. The effect is obviously hilarious.

> *Himself told himself 'You are charged for speeding.'*
> *Himself told himself, 'The policeman lie.'*

Spoiler's art was to start with the fantastic and to suggest its closeness to the texture of reality. Sparrow's art counterpoints Spoiler's in that it starts with the real and concrete political situation, and extracts the maximum absurdity from it. The two artists meet in their shared sense of the bizarre.

A calypso which resembles 'Police Get More Pay' in conception if not in complexity, is 'Mr Robinson and Lockjoint' (1964). Lockjoint was a contracting firm, which laid down a costly if necessary sewerage scheme in the early sixties. Sparrow's argument, an unanswerable one, was that people have to eat before a sewerage scheme can be of any use, but, 'The tax-man so fierce that the food getting scarce. Them pipes got to live on wind.'

The situation is again rich and complex. Legislation which was presumably meant to aid in the construction of the sewerage scheme, has placed such an extreme burden of taxation on the people, that they have to starve in order to pay the tax. This is the first assumption, as hyperbolical as any calypsonian's premises usually are. The second step follows from the first. Because the people are starving they have nothing to contribute to the sewerage scheme. It is another deadly circle of absurdity.

But Sparrow goes further than this, and points out that according to the logic of the first stanza and chorus, social status is directly proportional to the size of sewerage pipes. Only the wealthy have anything substantial to offer, in cash or kind, to a sewerage scheme. In fact, the bigger the man, the bigger the deposit.

Dem big big pipes dem does carry plenty load
Down Mucuarapo Road
The only impression that I got
St James people don't eat alot
Diego Martin ain't making fun
Is a good sized one
Just like in town
But Belmont and Laventille
Have the smallest sewerage pipe I ever see.

(*Whe you talking?*)
The people they got in Belmont
Also Laventille
Can't supply Lockjoint with nothing
In a quantity ... You see,
You have to buy food, you have to eat food
Before Lockjoint get something
But the tax-man so fierce
That the food getting scarce
Them pipes got to live on wind!

It is a devastating comment on social and economic disparity, and, in its peculiar way, a wry reflection on the society which permits this sort of thing to continue.

The final calypso which will be examined is the now famous satire on primary education in the West Indies, 'Dan is the Man in the Van'. This calypso is indispensable to any study of Sparrow as a 'poet', especially because here he consciously mocks at the way in which 'poetry' has been taught for several decades in the West Indies, while he simultaneously establishes and records his own tremendous 'folk poetry'. In other words, among other things, this calypso contrasts the enduring and ever-vital folk-oral tradition, with the unimaginative and irrelevant post-Victorian blood-sweat-and-tears system, which as part of the cultural front of Crown Colony Government, sought deliberately to destroy what remained of folk-ways and consciousness. One has only to read the school inspectors' reports for the first thirty years of the twentieth century, to understand how relentless was the Crown Colony struggle against the Creole language, consciousness and attitudes. When one remembers, too, the banning of drum, the laws against the Bongo dance, Shango, and Baptist religious observances; the unceasing attempts on the part of both Church and State to censor the calypso out of existence; and the fact that it was not until 1950, with the Shouters' Prohibition Repeal Ordinance that Black people enjoyed full freedom of worship; only then can one appreciate the full significance and beauty of a calypso like 'Dan is the Man in the Van', both as a vindication of the worth of the Creole self, and as a triumphant affirmation of the fact of survival, in spite of unremitting persecution by law, pulpit and the regimented irrelevance of an education system which (as Dickens shows in *Hard Times*), was geared to suit the simple brutal needs of an exploiting class.

Sparrow ridicules the entire system of learning by rote words which in the end reduce themselves to absurd questions such as 'Can a pig dance a jig for a fig?', to be met by the equally absurd and irrelevant response of the chorus 'Dan is the Man in the Van'. The implication is that neither questions nor answers were of any relevance in the calypsonian's, and by implication, the society's 'days at school'. A typical school inspector's report on reading in primary schools at the beginning of World War One (which is little different from reports long after the War) corroborates Sparrow's point. The Inspector lamented that even when the children achieved some fluency in Standard English, they never really grasped the sense of the words. 'The result is a dull uniform flow of words, almost as incomprehensible to the reader as to the hearer .... Mechanical sing-song accuracy without intelligent grasp of the meaning.' A little later, this same inspector commented on the recitation of poetry thus: 'A few teachers have an evident appreciation of beauty of thought and style, have endeavoured to convey it to their pupils and have taught them to recite with dainty feeling and graceful lightness.'

Since this latter quotation is an almost word for word repetition of a previous report by another hand, one can suppose that recitation 'with dainty feelings and graceful lightness' was then an ideal among colonial school inspectors in Trinidad.

It is at the monotony of slavish repetition that Sparrow mocks with a sort of dispassionate contempt, but 'dainty feelings' and graceful sing-song lightness are also subjected to laughter. The calypso begins with a general statement on the absurdity of the whole system of education.

According to the education you get when you small
You will grow up with true ambition and respect from one and all
But in my days at school
They treat me like a fool
The things they teach me I should be a block-headed mule.

Sparrow then launches an attack on the content of his education. What needs to be noted here is that the poems and nursery rhymes which he attacks seem to be drawn not merely from the English tradition but from fairly wide sources. There are Aesop's fables, West Indian and African folk tales — 'How the Agouti lose he tail and the Alligator trying to get monkey liver soup', 'Brer Rabbit', 'Morocoy with wings flying in the sky' — on the whole a fairly imaginative collection, even if the real purpose of the education was to inculcate a sense of loyalty to the British throne. The true focal point of the year was not the visit by the school inspector, but the Empire Day celebrations, when annual homage was paid to dead Queen Victoria. The more advanced poems in Cutteridge's West Indian Readers consciously sought to inculcate a love for the virtues of poverty, and Empire. In 'The Heritage', for example, West Indian children, themselves ravaged by malaria, hookworm and manutrition, were told that it was better to remain poor and healthy than to be rich and full of care. In another poem called 'Children of the Empire', they were taught to love the land that bore them, but the Empire best of all. In the introduction to 'Rule Britannia', the child learned that the sun never sets on the British Empire. Reports of school inspectors describe their consistent attempts to emphasize the idea of Empire. The World Wars were projected as wars in defence of the British Empire — which, of course, was not far from the truth as far as Britain was concerned.

Yet it was difficult to see how a Crown Colony education could be otherwise. Cutteridge's West Indian Readers of 1928 were the first attempt made to relate West Indian education, however imperfectly, to the West Indian environment. Only nationalist politics could bring about further change in the system, and, ironically, Cutteridge's Crown Colony readers are still in use in a number of schools in Independent Trinidad. But Sparrow doesn't directly attack the colonial nature of the education. He is not interested in doing justice to the content of Cutteridge's Readers. Instead he gratuitously confines his comments to the lessons of the first primer, and the dreary tedium of learning to read, spell, cypher, recite and sing by unimaginative rote.

Peter Peter was a pumpkin eater
And the Lilliput people tie Gulliver,
When I was sick and lay abed
I had two pillows at my head
The goose lay the golden egg ....

Satire is achieved here not through any attempt to render justice, or to point out the incongruity arising from fact itself, but through a consistent caricature, distortion and mockery; the exaggeration of certain selected elements in the readers to such an extent that the entire work of Cutteridge seems one vast and conscious attempt, not even to acculturate the Black West Indian to metropolitan values, but to make him into a comedian.

The poems and lessons they write and send from England
Impress me they were trying to cultivate comedians
Comic books make more sense
You know they are fictitious without pretence
J.O. Cutteridge wanted to keep us in ignorance.

The infants' introductory primer becomes the symbol of the entire education system of parrot-fashion platitude and post-Victorian absurdity. It is as if West Indian education were one long stuttering into language, punctuated by the sting

A carnival band on stage.

of the whip. Neither the child, nor the adult can quite recover from the bewildering shock of this stultifying process.

And he stood
in his shoes
and he won-
dered ....

The accenting of this last chorus sounds like the disjointed rhythms of some West Indian poetry. Broken rhythms are the logical results of the poet's sense of pained wonderment at the past he survived. In Sparrow, bewilderment is reinforced by the artistic use of mockery and mimesis. The complex irony of this calypso is only fulfilled in the last stanza, where the calypsonian explains how he finally escaped Cutteridge unscathed:

They wanted to keep me down indeed
They tried their best but didn't succeed
You see me head was duncy and up to now I can't read.

Natural stupidity, then, preserved him from becoming even more stupid. 'They beat me like a dog to learn that in school. If me head was bright I woulda been a damn fool.'

Somehow, deep truth is arrived at through distortion and the conscious quest for absurdity. When one bears in mind that at all levels Crown Colony education was irrelevant to West Indian nationhood, then one can interpret 'Dan is the Man in the Van' as an unintentional but accurate comment on the entire process of cultural imperialism, where only an inability to learn the full lesson of colonialism preserved some sense of self and direction in the colonized. Generally, those who were bright enough to learn the lesson of what Edward Braithwaite calls 'the cottonfields of Oxford', emerged scarred beyond recovery, asking absurd questions — 'Can a pig dance a jig for a fig?' — and receiving irrelevant answers — 'Dan is the Man in the Van' ... unable to move beyond the first lesson, the first stutter of independence.

There is more to the poetry of Sparrow's art than just this. For example, his best work has a telling precision of phrase which could only come from a highly sophisticated

Two ways of enjoying Tobago. The Mount Irvine golf course (bottom) is one of the finest in the Caribbean.

sense of the shades of possibility in words. In 'Drunken Moppers' (1965) he brilliantly satirizes imprecise use of language, and in the process mocks at the older tradition of 'robber-talk' in the 'picong' calypso. He has also sung in all the traditional forms of calypso except the now dead tradition of repartee, and done several different things better than most of his rivals can do the thing in which they specialize. He has been a master of tone of voice, brilliant at exploiting the dramatic 'I', and even at a complete masking, such as in 'Solomon Out'.

Finally, he has added fresh dimensions every year to the idea of form in calypso, precisely because he has been so alert to every influence, and also understands the roots from which the calypso sprang. These days, the forces which he has to integrate are immense. An international figure, he works in a parochial medium; a product of 1956 he has identified with the ruling party in Trinidad; risen from the grass-roots, he has now to span the gap between that world and the one he now occupies. The tension of all these conflicting forces has taken some toll, and there are signs of tiredness in his latest album, and a loss of rapport with the local audience. Also, much of the richness of language has disappeared. This may, however, be simply a bad year (1970). No one can tell with Sparrow, who, after all, has twice had to sing calypsoes denying his demise. Perhaps, long after his critics have buried him, he will be able to taunt them with the last lines of his 1959 classic, 'Simpson': 'The only disappointment is I ain't dead yet.'

Steelband

Pete Simon

De whole music world talking 'bout de steelband,
Experts cannot understand what dey hear,
Sweet, sweet music coming from out a steel pan,
Music that could make angels shed a tear,
It's so wonderful and rare.
Now let us take a real good look at de panman,
He's worth much more dan his weight in gold,
Oh what lovely music! What sweet expression!
It really does enrapture your very soul.
It's de gospel trute with no contradiction,
Now in song de real story can be told.

CHORUS

P-A-N, ping ping pong, ping pong, ping pong — Pan,
M-A-N, ping ping pong, ping pong, ping pong — Man,
De most inventive musician de whole world has ever seen,
If you know his history, you'll understand what I mean;
He rose from de dregs of society, to reach heights unseen.
P-A-N, Me-A-N — Pan-Man.

The above is the first verse and chorus of 'Tribute to the Panman' — a calypso composed and sung in the tents by the author during the 1971 Carnival season. Told in song was the story of the Evolution of the Steelband — a musical revelation! A fantastic innovation! Stupendous! Fabulous! Incredible! Musical experts have in fact run out of superlatives to describe this musical new dimension — the Steelband.

The steelband is, first and last, a product of Trinidad. It can be said to be a development of the tamboo-bamboo band, and, like many other forms of native expression, it met with stiff social and official displeasure. The stone which the builders rejected and relegated to the social dung-heap, has now become the cornerstone of the castle.

Many decades ago a ban was placed on the beating of drums during the carnival celebrations. Drums! Drums! Drums! The savage beat! The sensuous rhythm! The hidden messages of the talking drum: A son is born! A stranger in the land! The chief is dead! The enemy approaches! This is part and parcel of the cultural heritage of the Afro-West Indian, but the drums, so the authorities declared, exerted a most disturbing influence on carnival revellers. Their actions became uncontrollable, making them indulge in the worst excesses imaginable. And so the drums were banned.

But necessity is the mother of invention, and the resourceful ones lost no time in co-opting the bamboo. Pieces of bamboo of different lengths and sizes were cut at special times of the moon, and in the hands of these makeshift percussionists, were made to create the same atmosphere of primitive abandon. So was born the tamboo-bamboo band — from 'tambour', French for 'drum'.

In those days, the Band of the Year was not judged by panoply and visual impact as it is now, but by its offensive strength, the 'big pappies' in the band being renowned stickmen. Bloody battle was waged between contending bands, and fractured ribs, broken noses and split heads attested to the vigour and skill of those doughty wielders of wood. It was but natural that the tamboo-bamboo players lent support if and when the stickmen got into trouble.

Again, the authorities in their wisdom decided to impose a ban — this time on the tamboo-bamboo band on carnival days. The bands' activities were then confined to 'stick-yards' where, on afternoons, adventurous stickmen would gather and throw out the ringing challenge to all and sundry; 'Who is me fren don't come in de ring!'

After this ban, carnival revellers had perforce to content themselves with the scant support afforded by cuatro, flute, banjo, mandolin, violin, and clarinet and this went on for many years. The youngsters knew nothing about tamboo-bamboo, and the saxophone and trumpet became popular.

Then something happened. On Carnival Monday morning — *'Jour Ouvert'* — 1937, a band from New Town swept into the city. Paying tribute to the then current film hit, the banner proudly proclaimed *Alexander's Ragtime Band.* With branches waving in the air, a mass of jubilant humanity reacted ecstatically to its ample rhythm and noise.

All sorts of improvised percussion instruments had been co-opted by this band — buckets, dustbins, pitch-oil pans, soapboxes, motor-car hubs and other noise-making devices. Led by Lord Humbugger, a tall commanding figure dressed only in a top-hat and long black overcoat, it made a startling impact. Everybody jumped in. Passing bands quickly swelled the numbers, and when it reached Frederick Street, the main thoroughfare, nearly the whole city was jumping-up in Alexander's Ragtime Band. The clear, metallic ring of steel was the dominant feature of its sound.

The compelling rhythm had touched a hidden chord dormant all those years. The revellers recognized it as a call reaching out to them across centuries of time, and they responded to something which is indissolubly and inescapably part and parcel of their cultural and spriritual heritage. Alexander's Ragtime Band was the talk of the town.

Soon everybody got in on the act, and by the time carnival came around the following year, all the bands were selling rhythm and noise, while irate housewives were bewailing the loss of their dustbins.

Then came World War Two. The Japanese attack on Pearl Harbour and before that the US British Bases Agreement brought the American GI to Trinidad. Bases were established at Chaguaramas and Waller Field.* For security reasons carnival celebrations were suspended until the end of the war.

The pan boys did not take too kindly to this interference with their carnival festivities. 'Now, why dey must stop we Mas'?,' Big Brassy, a Hell-Yard stalwart fumed. 'If we aint play we mas' wid all dis war confusion, we bound to end up in de mad-house!' And the police had, perforce, to swoop

* The US negotiated with the British for bases in the Caribbean in early 1941. American armed forces came to Trinidad about August that year, some months before the Japanese attack on Pearl Harbour in December. The carnival, suspended in 1941, was resumed in 1946. Eds.

down on the more stubborn ones before they sullenly accepted the emergency measure.

But everyone had already been bitten by the bug. Although those were the days of rumours of submarines in the Gulf, of wailing sirens, of nightly black-outs, of the parasitic black-marketeer, and of the bread-line (which was not really a line but one mad scramble with the strongest getting more than their fill, while the 'decent ones' turned away in silent hunger) ... in spite of all this the pan adherents gathered during the day in their respective yards, gambled, 'skylarked' and promoted the necessary atmosphere of licence by beating their pans and their bits of steel.

The steelband is a city-born, slum-created phenomenon. Areas of subcultural living of known anti-social patterns, conspiring to promote all forms of social disease, readily come to mind — John John, East Dry River, Gonzales, Hell Yard, New Town. It is an open secret that such were the areas where expediency was the operative principle and futility the grinding philosophy; areas where children, for obvious reasons, could not hope to enjoy the luxury of the piano or the violin. It is not surprising, therefore, that people who as kids made their music from using a 'comb and paper' or a papaw stem or a bamboo flute, could readily make music out of steel pans.

But even among those lost souls, there were the dreamers, the visionaries, to whom the pans had offered a challenge. They experimented, and, in their quest to give a melodic form to the rhythms of the pans they soon discovered which ones had the best tonal qualities.

To Neville Jules, the leader of the Hell Yard Boys, goes deserved credit for native inventiveness. He divided the pan surface into a fournote compass in order to have it accommodate the popular calypso 'Whoopsin! Whoopsin!' This was treated in a crude, robust and primitive way, the only way then known. Other hands followed suit. By the time VE day dawned in 1945 with its jubilation, the melodic pan, simple in form, had arrived.

The people went mad with the joy of victory. Everybody — man, woman and child — swarmed into the streets, laughing, singing, shouting, dancing, jumping, chipping, shaking and 'wining'. Aided and abetted by the savage rhythm and noise of the modestly improved steelband — they more than made up for their enforced period of 'No Mas'', letting loose all their harnessed energy, singing 'Five years and eight months we ain't play no Mas'' to the tune of the old calypso 'Whole day, whole night Miss Marian'.

The cessation of hostilities was the signal for the lessening of the many emergency controls. There was a ceaseless round of celebrations. Dances, which usually ended at midnight, went right through to the next morning.

But tings wasn't always nice for our hero,
Society once treated him shamelessly,
Decent people shouted aloud, 'Oh no! no!
From dese hooligans, oh let us be free!
Dey implored de Holy Trinity.
Mothers warned their daughters about de panman,
Magistrates threw de whole book straight at dey head.
He was an outcast, a social infection,
You would be quite shocked at de tings dey said,
When de steelbands clashed it was murderation
Panmen did want to kill one another dead.

CHORUS

P-A-N, ping ping pong, ping pong, ping pong — Pan
Me-A-N, ping ping pong, ping pong, ping pong — Man
Some middle class never ever wanted de calypso or steelband
But when tings was ready-done den dey jump on de bandwaggon
But dat was expected in de old colonial tradition
P-A-N, Me-A-N — Pan-Man

The second verse and chorus of 'Tribute to the Panman' highlights the hazards which had, of necessity, to be endured by all forms of native expression.

As the island once more became carnival-conscious, steelbands began springing up like mushrooms all over the city and other centres of population. Every yard was a beehive of steelband activity and the residents of neighbourhoods hitherto peaceful were all up in arms against the unholy din. Complaints were voiced in the daily press and delegations were always at the doors of the authorities, begging for an end to it. To the so-called 'decent' people the steelband was the relic of a barbaric and primitive past, best forgotten; something that exasperated the fine susceptibilities of sensitive people. And strict instructions were laid down by well-meaning mothers 'not to go in those bad steelband yards'. Of course such warnings went unheeded, for there was a magnetic force in the pulsating rhythm which the youngsters could not resist.

Apart from the noise, it was the personnel of the bands which gave such offence — a veritable Rogues Gallery of bad-johns, switchblademen, pimps, touts and others whose penchant for violence caused 'decent people' to stampede for safety.

This was a nightmare period for probation officers and social welfare officers, and magistrates had no compunction in handing out stiff sentences to any panmen who found themselves in the dock on any charge at all. 'As long as you'se a steelband tess,' one chap wailed, 'a snowball in Hell have more chances dan you!'

Calypso was given much the same treatment. Both steelband and calypso had to run the gauntlet — from proscription to intolerance, to social disinheritance, to contempt, to snobbery and toleration, to patronage, to simulated acceptance, to full acceptance, and finally to total respect.

The reaction of the middle class (with a few exceptions quickly branded as 'black sheep') should not be seen as surprising or annoying. They were heavily compromised, the products of an era when it was considered a status symbol to frown upon native forms of cultural expression. Today the adherents of our native culture are no longer inmates of a colonially-initiated social concentration camp. Today the middle class supplies some of the standard-bearers at the head of the steelband parade. This is the law of natural consequence.

The wild American West of the Daltons and Jesse James and Billy the Kid, and the prohibition era of Chicago during the hey-day of Al Capone, Dion O'Bannion, Bugs

Moran and Dutch Schultz, spread their unsavoury influence to Trinidad during the violent period of steelband history. In those days steelband impact, like that of the tamboo-bamboo, depended not so much on 'panmanship' (which was still rather elementary) as on the strong-arm squad among its exponents. Every dance hall in the city became an amphitheatre where members and supporters of rival bands, using all available weapons, swarmed into one another as dancers and musicians alike scampered for safety. And on carnival days revellers and spectators alike went through a purgatory of apprehension as they ventured forth into the national festival, hoping against hope that they would be somewhere else when 'de bacanal start'.

The epic clash between Invaders and Tokyo on Carnival Tuesday afternoon, 1956, has been immortalised by Lord Blakie in his famous calypso, 'The Steelband Clash!'

It was bacanal! Ah ha!
In de Carnival! Ah ha!
Fight for so, wid Invaders and Tokyo
And when de two bands clash
Mamayo, if you see cutlash
Never me again
To jump-up in a steelband in Port of Spain.

Never me again! Many people vowed this! But this was just wishful thinking or, as Trinidadians say, 'gran-charge', for came next carnival and the infectious rhythm of steel made liars of them as they eagerly awaited their Jouvert jump-up on Monday morning and their 'Las-Lap' on Tuesday night, hoping against hope that nothing untoward would happen.

But all dese happenings were part of an era
A time of defiance and blood and sand
For only de real low-class kinda creatures
With a grim, grim determination
In de grass-roots culture tradition
Soon de panman transformed into a musician
Who took great pride in Panology
Interpreting de great masters with distinction

Just like Philharmonic Symphony
And beating out their calypso with abandon
On Carnival days with vigour and energy

CHORUS

P-A-N, ping ping pong, ping pong, ping pong — Pan
Me-A-N, ping ping pong, ping pong, ping pong — Man
Unofficial ambassadors dat is what everybody say
Doing a mighty better job dan de Tourist Board any day
What greater advertisement, Tripoli wid Liberace
P-A-N, Me-A-N — Pan-Man.

The third verse and chorus of 'Tribute to the Panman' tells the underlying reasons for the eventual success of the steelband.

Thank the Almighty there is such a thing as native culture or this would have been a most dreary, monotonous and humdrum world. Thank the Almighty that this culture is the handiwork and inalienable property of 'those people' — the disinherited, the denizens of the grass-roots, the poor, the peasants, the labourers, the social pariahs, the flotsam and jetsam of society; people who are blessed with some hidden compensatory component which gives them guts, intensity of purpose and determination to protect them against the disintegrating forces of a hypocritical society. Thank the Almighty that such people were the progenitors of the steelband. The other kind — those whose lives are ruled by the perpetual question 'What will decent people say?' — would have chickened out long ago in the face of so much social and official displeasure.

And now, having emerged from the social catacombs, the panman is crashing every musical barrier in a manner that would make members of any Philharmonic Symphony Orchestra blush with envy. The biennial Steelband Festival highlights his wizardry. This is his 'shining hour', when for a period of three weeks or so, all the leading bands vie with one another, to be judged 'Festival Champs', by outstanding music adjudicators — many of them of international repute.

Here the great composers — Schubert, Bach, Beethoven and others of this illustrious company — are given attention with marks awarded for stage appearance, discipline, tonality, adherence to score, orchestration, shades and nuances of expression. What a far cry from Alexander's Ragtime Band and the hooliganism of yesteryear!

Unofficial Ambassadors! This is the tribute paid to the steelbandsmen of the country; for they have appeared in nearly all the major cities of the world: London, New York, Paris, Montreal and Toronto, Los Angeles, Berlin, Caracas, Rio, and many others. They have played at Radio City Music Hall and at the famous Carnegie Hall. They have appeared on the Ed Sullivan Show in New York. They have astounded the patrons of the Las Vegas night clubs and 'The Sands' in Nevada. They have even had engagements on Russian cruise ships plying between Trinidad and Northern Europe.

And Trinidad Tripoli band is now the main attraction on the programme of famous pianist-showman, Liberace, as they go on their record-breaking tour of top places of entertainment and the University circuit of the United States.

De boss of dem all is de great pan-tuner,
Who gives de notes to de old steel pans,
He never ever had a musical teacher,
But just by using his ears and hands,
He had brought such great fame to dis land.
And if it wasn't for dis ting dey call steelband,
De police and dem woulda have it hard,
So much discipline, so much concentration,
De panmen does expend in de steelband yard,
After practising, dey near to exhaustion,
What a blessing in disguise for Trinidad!

CHORUS

P-A-N, ping ping pong, ping pong, ping pong — Pan
Me-A-N, ping ping pong, ping pong, ping pong — Man
We need a steelband Hall of Fame,
Honouring de giants of Pan
Neville Jules and Patsy Haynes, Elie Mannette and 'Spree' Simon,
Tony Williams and Oscar Pile, Bertie Marshall and Andrew Pan
P-A-N, Me-A-N — Pan-Man.

A steelband today has pans of all ranges and depths — oil drums have been found to be best suited for the purpose of making these instruments. There are many different kinds of pan now in use. The leading pans which supply the melody are the Ping Pong or Soprano pans, with twenty-eight to thirty-two notes, embracing both the diatonic and chromatic scales. The background or harmony pans are the Alto pans, Tenor pans, Guitar pans, Cellos and Basses. And of course there is the rhythm section — the percussionists with drums and cymbals and scratchers (*cucarachas*), and most important of all, the steel or iron men, the chaps who beat out the rhythm which gives the distinctive metallic thrust to the steelbands on carnival days.

Except for the Basses, the pans are cut to required sizes, and the unopened ends sunk to a certain level by a five-pound sledge-hammer — quite unlike the early days when they were beaten outwards, convex instead of concave. The pan is then placed on a blazing wood fire for some thirty or forty minutes after which oil is thrown on it in order to temper the steel. The required notes are then marked on the surface and the tuner sets to work with hammer and cold chisel.

Pan-tuning is an art of amazing natural musical skill, bordering on genius. Orthodox musicians are always rendered speechless at the range of tonal shades and nuances within the compass of the various pans.

To see a pan-tuner at work is a revelation of intensity bordering on spiritual abstraction, astonishing to see in a sometimes crude and illiterate man who in nine cases out of ten, knows not a single note of written music. What a refined ear! What artistry!

Pan-tuners are at a premium and are now being offered the most attractive inducements by other countries who for obvious reasons hope to develop and promote the steelband for all it is worth for their own benefit. Even the United States seems to be embarking on a long-range steelband programme and has employed some of our pan-tuners.

Trinidad can probably boast of being the most musical place under the sun; for the steelband has actually become a Trinidadian way of life. A metallic note greets the ear of the new-born and conditions his musical appetite; and ping-pong prodigies aged six and seven are sometimes featured as soloists in top bands.

One can hardly keep track of the innumerable steelbands, each under a distinctive name, which strut across the steelband stange. Every village or hamlet can boast of between two and four bands vying for supremacy. In the larger centres a sizeable percentage of the panmen are college and high-school students and white-collar workers. To be a Giant Panman is the ambition of many a teenager, of whatever class. Times have really changed!

Astute observers are unanimous in the view that the steelband is a great instrument of social control which, over the past few years, has unwittingly been supplementing the work of the police. The concentration and discipline displayed by panmen in committing to memory the many intricate arrangements of calypso and — above all — the classic masterpieces of the great composers, could only be the result of dedication, application and considerable self-involvement. This, truly, is a blessing in disguise for Trinidad and Tobago. Bearing in mind the dictum, 'The Devil finds mischief still for idle hands to do,' the prospect of thousands of strong, energetic young men roaming the streets, especially at nights, with no socially-reinforcing activity, is an alarming one.

The co-opting of the steelband as a buffer in the fight against juvenile delinquency was brought into focus some years ago when the Steelband Association of Trinidad and Tobago and our Tourist Board, hit upon the novel idea of exposing school-children, especially those from areas with high delinquency rates, to the self-involving exercise of learning to play the pans during the 'long hot summer' school holidays. Martin Albino, one of our top-flight exponents of the Pan, was given such an assignment. It was a resounding success — the kids needed no coaxing.

Pan in Church? Sounds like Mission Impossible! But that which was once called a 'prelude to Armageddon' is now setting the tone and atmosphere for conversation with God. The steelband has played at the services of several church organizations in Trinidad, and the once socially disinherited panmen now walk with a new-found dignity and wear their craft as a status symbol, a badge of distinction!

In the welter of contending claims to be founders of the Empire of Pan, the following personalities are outstanding: Neville Jules, and 'Fish-eye' Olivierre of Hell Yard, now Trinidad All Stars; Winston 'Spree' Simon of John John; Elie Mannette of Invaders; Sonny Roach of Sun Valley; Oscar Pile and Patsy Haynes of Casablanca, and Andrew 'Pan' De Labastide and 'Patch-eye' Pajotte of Hill Sixty.

Who earned the distinction of being the first man to beat out a recognized tune on the pan has always been a subject of dispute. But two names keep cropping up — Neville Jules of Hell Yard who tapped out the notes to a then well-known calypso 'Whoopsin! Whoopsin!' and Winston 'Spree' Simon who also has been credited with beating out 'Mary had a Little Lamb'.*

What a timid beginning to an art which would soon encompass the masterpieces of Bach and Beethoven, Wagner and Mozart, Tchaikovsky, Dvorak and others.

But the story of pan has not yet been fully told. As time marches on, the imaginative ones are setting their sights on new and loftier steelband horizons. Tony Williams of North Stars, Bertie Marshall of Highlanders and Rudolph Charles of Gay Desperados have, all along, been experimenting to improve the tonal qualities of Pan, and many are the instrumental innovations which have been accredited to these three.

No one can long resist the pulsating rhythm of the steelband; and visitors to the Trinidad Carnival always marvel at the sight of thousands of masqueraders — chipping, dancing and shaking their bodies in time to the compelling beat of bands sometimes comprising two hundred pans and one hundred and fifty instrumentalists. So irresistible is the music's attraction that, quite unconsciously, they soon find

* Winston 'Spree' Simon claims association with the *China Town* or *John John* Band since 1937. He also claims to be the first steelbandsman to put a set of notes on pan, and play the first complete tune: such simple tunes as 'Mary had a Little Lamb'; and game-songs like 'River-vine Cuvali', and 'Sally, Sally Water'. He was a steelband tutor in 1956/1957 in Nigeria and Ghana, under a sponsorship programme by the Mobile Oil Company. Eds.

themselves on the fringe of the band and then in the thick of things.

'How de heck do you people dance so darn well?' one of them wanted to know. 'Even the three-years olds are experts!'

'Bredder,' one chap set him right, 'You have to be born wid it. Nobody can't show you how. You must born wid rittum in your blood!'

Cricket

C. L. R. James

Quanko Samba in *The Pickwick Papers*, the slave who bowled himself to death on behalf of his master, was a Jamaican. But it seems pretty certain that right through the Caribbean, Trinidad included, the slaves were incorporated in the game of cricket by their masters, probably as fast bowlers.

Slavery was abolished in 1834, and my father, born in 1876, rapidly became the great batsman of our village, Tunapuna. There lived there maybe one or two thousand people, poverty-stricken but living a Western type of life. There was nothing native in the West Indies. The native Amerindians had been killed off.

The island is 50 miles long and 30 miles broad, and I cannot remember a little village anywhere where there was not an empty space and a cricket pitch in the centre.

My father was a member of cricket club which had been formed by the young men of the area, who used the new overarm instead of the old underarm bowling. But another team in the area still bowled underarm. So they professed great contempt for the new-fangled players, who played overarm, and kept to their underarm bowling. The overarm bowlers challenged them to a match. The older ones refused.

Even in those days there was a cricket competition every Saturday, organized from Port of Spain. From Tunapuna, the underarm players and my father's team both joined. Thus, they had to play against one another after all.

My father was a teacher, and the head of his school was a man called Mr Waddell, a great underarm cricketer in his day, but he sided with my father's team. Every afternoon, after school, he had the senior boys bowling to my father, while he bowled underarm, the kind of bowling my father

The Muslim celebration of Hosein.

NO
ENTRY

would have to meet. Friday afternoon, Mr Waddell told my father, 'Robert, open out now and make your strokes.'

On the match day great numbers of people came around to see the competition between the older generation and the new. My father went in first wicket down, made forty-eight not out, and they beat the old gentlemen by eight wickets.

One of the older generation was Mr Blenman, the butcher. Mr Blenman did not play cricket any more but he told my father gravely, 'Robert, we're not finished with it. We'll play you another match one day.' My father was triumphant: 'Whenever you are ready.'

After a year or two Mr Blenman informed my father his team was now ready to play a challenge match. As usual many of the neighbourhood turned up for the match. In Mr Blenman's team was a stranger.

He batted and batted. Ninety-five runs. And he would have made a hundred but that he got run out at ninety-five. Worse still; when the young men went in to bat the stranger bowled almost as well, and the older generation won the match in great style. My father's team wondered who the stranger was. And only a year or two afterwards when the West Indian team was chosen to go to England they learnt that Mr Brenman's stranger was C.A. Ollivierre, one of the famous family of cricketers from St Vincent. It seems that Mr Blenman had probably paid his passage from St Vincent and then back again. Ollivierre distinguished himself greatly in England. Such was the temper of cricket in a West Indian village nearly a hundered years ago.

Another story which will explain what cricket meant to the ordinary population of those days. The late Lord Constantine's father was one of the great cricketers of the day. He was always included in an all West Indian team. In 1900 H.G.B. Austin organized a trip of West Indian cricketers to England. Naturally Constantine was selected. But in those days the player paid his own passage and stood his own expenses. On the day that the boat was to leave Trinidad Constantine was seen walking about dejectedly in Port of Spain.

Friends came up anxiously to ask him, 'Cons, what is happening?' 'Old Cons' replied, 'I have no money to pay

Top: Carting cane.
Bottom: Cattle grazing.

my passage. I have no clothes and no expenses. I told them I can't go and am staying here.'

One of the local merchants, a coloured man, went around to various people to make a collection. 'Old Cons' was provided with some new clothes, a bat or two and money for expenses. And they rushed down to the wharf.

But the launch to take them to the boat had already left. They hired a fast launch and caught the ship before it left the Gulf. 'Old Cons' scrambled on board and hit the first century at Lord's of a West Indian cricketer.

I used to play in local matches in addition to matches of the regular competition, and one thing was noticeable. But all matches were always serious. The kind of jovial game that used to be played among English villages was unknown to us. It was unknown in Trinidad, and if it was unknown in Trinidad it was certainly not known in Barbados. When you played a match you fought it out to the end. That was the milieu which produced the many brilliant West Indian players of the last quarter of a century.

We played those days with a matting wicket. The matting cost money. Bats cost money. Balls cost money. You needed money to pay the fare of the teams from one village to another village. Everybody liked to play in white pants and white shoes. Quite often a fine young player did not have the money to pay his expenses or even his fare. Quite often a local cricket magnate, black, East Indian or Chinese, took the team under his patronage, paid up what was needed, and when they won a match spent money on a general fête. Cricket was one of the means whereby the general population of the West Indies incorporated into their ways of life and thinking much of the style and manners inherent in the English way of life.

In the thirties, when Trinidad played against Barbados, or against the MCC, the island teams consisted of people of all the different races who constituted the population. But in our island games it was not like that. Every section of the population had its own type of cricket club. There was, for example, the Queens Park Club which was the club of the white people, the merchants, the government officials and, rarely, a black man who had enough money and enough status to be included in that team. The Shamrock Club consisted of white Roman Catholics who were a very strong group in the island. Then, playing the competition matches, there was another club, the Constabulary, consisting of policemen, chiefly black men, captained by a white officer. In the big first-class competition there was another club, Stingo. Stingo consisted of the butcher, the baker, the candlestick maker, plebeians in the town and some who came in from the country. They were very fine cricketers but their social status was not high. And there was another team that consisted of black people who were not plebeians, but law clerks, teachers, government civil servants. Then there was yet another team, the Maple Club. In those days it consisted of people of brown skin, from that important brown-skinned Caribbean middle class who played such a role in the past history of the islands and whose influence continued until a very few years ago. (In fact some people say they still exercise a certain amount of influence, although it is not nearly as strong as it used to be.) All this is important in regards to the cricket we played, in that players felt they represented the particular section of society from which their team came. Thus Stingo, the plebeians, played a very hard game against Shannon, the black lower middle class. The Maple brown-skinned club, the black-skinned plebeians of Stingo and the Shannon lower middle class played very hard against the white clubs. We wanted to show them who and what we were. And for much the same reason we played very hard against one another. In general, the population which came to see these games supported chiefly the Shannon Club. Things could be very tense in important games. Although we were playing cricket, the social qualities of the different clubs we represented, and certain social conflicts, or at least differences, were expressed very sharply in the cricket matches of the islands. Now that has to be noted because when we got together to play an island from outside, or to play an English team that was visiting us, we didn't have much of these differences. Certain of the upper classes gained certain advantages, but by and large the island team often gave a general picture of the population.

Let me say at once that we didn't fight or squabble in any unsportsmanlike way. We just played, knowing that we were representing far more than the actual game. And this sort of representation could be found all over the island.

There were places in the island where there was a team of East Indians, and I know that many years before I began to play there was a team of Chinese. These teams would play together without hostility and at the end of the game celebrate with drinks of rum after playing very hard; and altogether, although there was this constantly savage competition, the standard of sportsmanship was extremely high.

To show how the manners and style of West Indian life were affected by the manners and style of cricket, would, I believe, be going beyond what can reasonably be attempted in a brief sketch. Still, we were all affected by the game and I think that one story will show how deeply and unexpectedly it affected me.

It was the biggest of all games when the MCC visited the West Indian islands one by one. Almost as important was when one island team, Trinidad, played another, Barbados. Barbados in the thirties, and even before that, had two great batsmen, George Challenor and Percy Tarilton. Challenor was not only a great player. He was the idol of the whole West Indies, particularly after he had visited England in 1923 and showed himself if not better, at least not inferior to the great English batsmen of the day.

So one day in the late 1920s, Barbados was playing against Trinidad. Trinidad won the toss and batted the greater part of the first day. Thus in the last fifteen or twenty minutes Challenor and Tarilton opened for Barbados. The umpire was Toby Creighton. Toby was a coloured man, light-skinned, one of the very few coloured men who had been admitted to one of the white clubs, the Shamrock Club. He spoke well, was full of information, extremely well-educated, and was altogether a man of social parts. Included among these was being an umpire in the big game although he himself did not play.

Playing for Trinidad was Arthur Waddell (and to show how close things were and still are in the islands, Waddell was the youngest son of the same Mr Waddell who had prepared my father for the big match in Tunapuna of which we have spoken). Young Waddell was the captain of the team for which I played and I knew his bowling well. I used to be second slip to Waddell when he opened the bowling for our side.

So this day I placed myself behind the white board usually placed there to prevent the batsmen from being disturbed by passers-by. From behind the white board you could really see the play and for me this was important, both as a devotee and as a sports correspondent. Waddell began bowling to Challenor. I knew what he was going to do and he did it. The first two balls he bowled outside the off-stump, rather short, to get his length and know exactly what he was doing. I knew what would happen with the next three balls.

They were dead straight on the centre wicket, of good length and the batsman could do nothing else but defend. And then came the last ball of the over. This ball began outside the leg stump and remained there for some time. It was a well-pitched up ball. Challenor put his left foot forward and got ready to glance the ball down to the leg boundary. For most of the way the ball remained outside the leg stump, then it ducked down to the wicket. Challenor missed his stroke entirely and the ball hit his leg right in front of the wicket.

A shout went round the ground: 'How's that?' In those days everybody appealed whenever the ball hit an opposing batsman's foot. I, however, knew Waddell's bowling as well as anybody else. I had seen him often enough open exactly in this way. Standing behind the white board I saw what happened and my appeal was perhaps the most genuine of all. But Creighton, the umpire, very firmly shook his head and said, 'No.' And Challenor continued his innings.

A few days afterwards I met Creighton. He and I used to talk. So I began rather abruptly: 'But Toby, you know that Challenor was out in that first over when Waddell hit his foot.'

Toby replied immediately in his quick firm speech: 'Of course Challenor was out.'

'But why didn't you give him out?' I asked.

He replied: 'Nello, I am surprised at you. You wanted me, with fifteen minutes to go, in a match of Trinidad versus Barbados, to put Challenor out, LBW for nought in the first over? I thought you were a person of more sophistication than that.'

I began to see his point. He took advantage of my uncertainty and asked me: 'Would you have given him an out?'

I could not answer. And there I have to leave it. The episode showed that not only Toby but I too, a cricked correspondent and a man of irrefutable rectitude when it came to cricket decisions, had to think twice about this one. Giving a great man like Challenor out in the first over LBW, in a Trinidad versus Barbados match, was just something we did not do in the West Indies.

Nor does this tale end here. Many years after, when we had become the equals of any other players in the world, Constantine*, the great fast bowler, would tell me how in Test matches he repeatedly saw great opening batsmen given not out in the opening overs when he, at any rate, was quite certain they were out. I doubt, however, if the umpires would have spoken as plainly about it as Toby spoke to me. There is more of West Indian cricket and West Indian social relations in that curious episode than I have the space to point out.

* Later Baron Constantine of Maravel and Nelson.

East Indian Life and Culture

Brinsley Samaroo

After the abolition of both slavery in 1834 and the apprenticeship system which followed it in 1838, many of the freed Africans deserted the plantations of Trinidad. This was partly because the plantations represented the scene of their long degradation which they now wished to forget, and partly because of the planters' refusal or inability to grant an increase in wages. In Trinidad and what was then British Guiana, where there were large areas of uncultivated lands on which the former slaves could settle, the effects of this desertion were particularly ruinous. At first unsuccessful attempts were made to introduce an alternative labour supply from south-western Europe, China and the United States of America; later indentured East Indian labour was successfully introduced. The first group of East Indians arrived in Trinidad in 1845 and by 1917, when the system of indentured Indian immigration ended, just over one hundred and forty-three thousand labourers had been brought over. Today the East Indians form about thirty-nine percent of Trinidad's population of just under one million.

The system of indentureship meant, very briefly, that the East Indian had to sign a bond to stay in the service of a particular planter for five years. During this period he was paid a small wage and supplied with the basic necessities of life such as housing, articles of clothing, cooking utensils and sometimes a small plot of land on which he could grow vegetables for daily use. At the end of the period of indentureship the East Indian was encouraged to re-indenture himself by the offer of a bonus for each year of renewed indentureship. Alternatively, he could either take advantage of the offer of a free return passage to India, or he could become owner of a piece of land which he could start to cultivate on his own account.

The Indians who came to the Caribbean were mostly of those castes whose functions included agricultural work. Members of the highest or Brahmin caste came chiefly as priests and teachers, and the British immigration authorities did their utmost to discourage the indentureship of men of the Tschatriya or warrior caste. Hence the majority of those who came belonged to the Vaishya or Shudra castes. It is also interesting to note that most of those who came from India came from the north-eastern part of that country — from areas which correspond today to the States of Uttar Pradesh, Bengal and Bihar — and from the southern state of Madras. In these areas the main crops grown are rice, sugar-cane and pulses, and cattle are reared on a large scale. Coming as they did from an agricultural environment, the East Indians soon adapted themselves to their new surroundings, often introducing new species of plants and of animals to the Caribbean, and improving existing cultivation by using new techniques. They made rice popular in the region and introduced new methods of irrigation to its production; they introduced new breeds of cattle, the water buffalo, for example, and a wide variety of food and ornamental plants well suited to Caribbean conditions. If the opinion of a visitor to Trinidad in 1859 can be taken as an indication of the impact of the East Indians on the economy of Trinidad, one can conclude that it was considerable. W.G. Sewell in *The Ordeal of Free Labour in the West Indies* (1861) points out that 'Not only has the island been saved from impending ruin, but a prospect of future prosperity opened to her such as no British island in these seas ever before enjoyed under any system, slave or free.'

Intermingling and interaction among East Indians at the recruiting depots in India, and on the ships, led to modifications of caste, family and religious patterns. There were further modifications on the plantations and as the East Indians became educated in Christian schools in Trinidad. Regulations on the ship, for example, paid scant attention to caste distinctions and often people of different castes had to sleep in the same area, eat similar food and use common facilities. Further inroads into the caste system were made when lower caste immigrants, desiring to make a fresh start in life in a community where they were not known, claimed that they were members of a higher caste than their own, thus gaining acceptance at a higher social level. But if the caste system underwent dilution it was replaced by a new bond of unity: the brotherhood of the boat or 'Jahaji bhai'. This meant that all those who came on the same boat were brothers irrespective of caste, and their descendants, even at the present time, maintain this brotherhood. The Indian system of village organization, the panchayat, was also brought from the villages of north-eastern India. The panchayat was a five-man council of elders which ran the affairs of the village and arranged its economic and social activities. In Trinidad, however, the inter-racial nature of many of the villages and the ease with which the central government could administer the rural communities made the panchayat system as practised in India inapplicable. Today there are very few of these organizations, but where they do remain they exercise a strong moral authority.

More permanent aspects of Indian life very evident in Trinidad are Indian food, the language of north and central India — Hindi — and the two major religions of the subcontinent, Islam and Hinduism. Indian curries in all their spice-laden varieties can be found in most Trinidad homes. The *dhalpouri* is as popular a late-night snack* as are fish and chips in European cities, and the importance of rice as one of the staples of the Trinidad diet is a direct result of East Indian influence. Vegetable markets in Chaguanas or San Fernando seem to be transported replicas of the open-air markets of Patna or Madras, and the itinerant nut and candy-sellers of Trinidad's main thoroughfares ply their trade in exactly the same way as their counterparts in large Indian cities. Hindi continues to be one of the secondary languages spoken in Trinidad and a number of words that have come into common usage — pundit, mango, bungalow — are derived from this language. In a similar

* Also popularly presented for sale is *roti*, with different kinds of curried meats. Eds.

way, many of the place-names in Trinidad are direct importations from India — Fyzabad, Coromandel, Madras Settlement, Barrackpore.

The fact that Hindi and Urdu continue to be used in Trinidad is due largely to the observance of Oriental religions by more than fifty percent of Trinidad's East Indians. Since Islamic and Hindu religious practices are conducted mainly in Urdu and Hindi, these languages have been kept alive. Followers of the Islamic faith hold their namaaz or prayers in mosques of exquisite design which are found chiefly in the area that extends from St Joseph to Barataria. The Shiah sect of this faith also celebrate the Muharram or Husain festival each March with great enthusiasm. The Husain celebration commemorates the death of Mohammed's descendant Husain who was killed at the battle of Kerbela in 680 AD. Intricately decorated taziyas (tombs) are built during the weeks preceding the celebration and on the night of the festival these taziyas, symbolic representations of the tombs of Husain and his brother Hassan, are carried through the streets to the accompaniment of vigorous drum-beating. The procession pauses at certain points where prayers are said for the repose of the souls of these saints, and the taziyas are finally consigned to a river or to the sea. During recent years this and other East Indian celebrations have attracted large numbers of non-Indians who are becoming increasingly conscious of their significance.

The Hindus, who form the largest part of Trinidad's East Indian community, observe their thanksgiving, or puja ceremonies in a manner that is hardly different from that of contemporary India or, indeed, from that of the ancient Vedic period of history. From India the Hindu brought the saddhu, or priest, who officiates at religious functions, and the sacred tulsi plant and the pipal leaf, both of which are used in the ceremonies of thanksgiving. Offerings are made to the various deities; the Satya Narain Puja, for example, is done to the god of truth, and Suraj Puja to the solar deity. At the end of each puja a flag or jhandi is planted in front of the devotee's home to commemorate the ceremony of thanksgiving. To the non-Christian East Indian religion is the focal point of life. He does not make the distinction between religion and politics or between religion and social life that Western civilization makes. The religious observance of the East Indian is at the same time a social occasion, so the East Indian festivals which span the entire year, each in its season, are as social as they are religious. These festivals are occasions when old friends renew their friendship, when new ones are made, when business deals are discussed and when marriages are arranged. From the East Indian point of view these festivals correspond to the carnival celebrations that take place in Trinidad during the month of February in which the participants are drawn mainly from the non-East Indian section of the population.

Possibly the best known of these religious-*cum*-social festivals is that of Ramleela, which takes place during late October or early November each year. The source of this celebration is the Ramayana, an epic written in Bengal some four centuries before Christ. Ram, heir to the throne of Oudh, is deprived of his birthright by a jealous stepmother who secures his banishment into a forest. Ram and his wife Sita settle in their new environment, but Sita is soon abducted by Ravanna, the king of Lanka (believed to be modern Ceylon). Ram wages a long and bitter battle against Ravanna, finally defeats him and rescues Sita. The couple then return to Oudh after an absence of some fourteen years and Ram is restored to the throne. The festival of Deya Dewali, which inaugurates the Ramleela celebrations, celebrates Ram's return from the forest. Small earthen crucibles (deyas) are lighted and placed along pathways and around houses to give light to the returning hero. During the fortnight that follows different cultural groups enact various sections of the Ramayana story and the celebration ends with the burning of an effigy of Ravanna — a symbolic victory of the forces of good over those of evil.

Besides these general celebrations, Trinidad's Moslems and Hindus celebrate particular occasions like births, marriages or a good harvest. East Indian marriages, especially, are celebrated on a grand scale. To the East Indian the marriage of a son or a daughter is a time of joy and this joy must be shared as widely as possible. So the parents of the bride and of the groom generally invite the entire village to the celebration as well as hundreds of guests from adjacent districts. Festivities, often lasting weeks, are held both at the bride's and at the bridegroom's homes and on the day of the wedding a meal is shared by all the celebrants first at the bride's residence and later at the bridegroom's. This form of community marriage celebration, accompanied by drum-beating and loud music, contrasts markedly with the quieter, smaller weddings of Trinidad's Christian community.

There is also a substantial number of Christian East Indians, the majority of the Presbyterian faith. The fact that most Christian Indians are Presbyterian is due to the sustained proselytizing and educational work done by the Presbyterian Canadian missionaries who started a church and a school at Iere village in South Trinidad in 1868. The East Indians, whose educational needs had been largely overlooked in a system of education where the medium of instruction was English, readily accepted the Canadian missionaries who learnt Hindi and taught in that language. By the early twentieth century the Canadian missionaries had established primary schools in many parts of the island, the heaviest concentration being in the sugar growing areas. By this time, too, they had established two secondary schools one for boys and the other for girls, and a teacher training college in San Fernando. Given this system of education and conversion, many Muslims and Hindus became Presbyterians. They saw in conversion a means of obtaining education and consequently economic benefits in a society where the possession of a western education was the passport to employment. Others saw Christianity and western education as means of becoming active in the agitation for political concessions which gained momentum from the late nineteenth century. Trinidad's Christian Indians, then, because of these influences, have become highly westernized or, as some prefer to describe them, they have become 'Indo-Saxons'. Most of them participate in national celebrations like Carnival, and they are often culturally indistinguishable from the non-Indian section of the population.

The pattern of East Indian population distribution laid down during the period of indentureship remains basically the same, although improved communications and better education have brought about some changes. The majority of East

Indians live in rural areas, and those rural areas which are the main producers of sugar cane and rice are the major areas of concentration of East Indians. This rural concentration has had the unfortunate effect of preventing contact between the two major races of Trinidad — the East Indians and the people of African descent. The marked dissimilarity between Oriental religions and Christianity, which is adhered to by the majority of the non-East Indian populations, has served also to make the separateness of the two communities more marked. This separateness is manifested at various points in the society. Persons of African descent for example, having pursued the professions of law and medicine, nevertheless, have a preference for clerical and administrative jobs in the Civil Service and elsewhere, and in the Police and Defence Forces; whereas the East Indian, having also pursued the said professions, has sought to occupy more independent positions like farming, shopkeeping, and other business ventures. Another area of activity where this difference is noticeable is in politics. More than a century of separateness has dictated a largely separate pattern of development for the two major ethnic groups. In the late nineteenth century the East Indians formed their own political pressure groups such as the East Indian National Association and the East Indian National Congress, whereas Trinidad's people of African descent formed the Workingmen's Association and the Pan African Association. During the last two decades many attempts have been made to bridge this gap and whilst these have not totally succeeded, they have served to reduce inter-racial friction to a considerable degree. At the present time the East Indians in the Parliament are mainly representatives from rural agricultural communities whereas the mainly non-Indian urban areas are predominantly represented by persons of African descent.

All this does not mean that there are no areas of inter-racial co-operation or harmonious co-existence. Examples of East Indians in the Civil Service or in the Police Force are by no means rare, nor is it impossible to find East Indians in a predominantly non-East Indian political party or vice versa. At the St Augustine campus of the University of the West Indies there are groups of undergraduates who spend considerable time discussing the problem of making Trinidad and Tobago a genuinely multi-racial society, and this interest is reflected in the number of research projects which are exploring this subject. Additionally the number of non-East Indians taking part in the religious festivals of the Hindus and Moslems seems to indicate that new areas of co-operation are being gradually explored.

The presence of East Indians in Trinidad and Tobago offers this society the opportunity as well as the challenge of creating out of disparate elements and diverse cultures a coherent pattern of life. The blending of the Orient with fragments of an African and a European past can produce a fascinating and a unique society. And in a world where the problem of racial difference is threatening to cleave our civilization in twain, this experiment can have valuable lessons for others. There are signs that a solution will be reached in Trinidad.

Brave Buildings

Architecture in Trinidad and Tobago

John Newel Lewis

No! Trinidad is not an extension of Europe and not a branch of it. Architecturally I admit it appears to be a conglomerate of styles plucked from the European scene, but somehow along the line the buildings have become Trinidadian and that is what is important. Good Trinidad architecture has panache, style, scale and a social sense. It has two façades, one face presenting itself boldly to the world, the other worn down by a tropical existence and primaeval decay. The brave buildings rise against a rapacious nature and struggle to survive the decades.

In Port of Spain the Public Transport Company operates a two-hour sight-seeing tour on Saturdays, leaving from the Old Railway Building, South Quay. It makes an excellent introduction to the city. Check times of departure and price of ticket (sold on the coach) with The Tourist Board, 56 Frederick Street, Port of Spain. The buildings succeed in creating an urban environment which is becoming more sophisticated. Air conditioning is the key as the town readjusts. But the past still surrounds us.

Observe the Roman Catholic Cathedral at the end of Independence Square, with its twin Gothic revival towers. Further up on Frederick Street historic Woodford Square is flanked by the Red House, a huge red inedible cake in the Renaissance style which is the seat of Government, and the Gothic Anglican Holy Trinity Cathedral, of 1823 vintage, but in a beautiful setting. Other interesting buildings pop up amidst the rebuilding of the old town, including the occasional white Indian building in the Indo-Grecian style and 'Knowsley', a house on the Savannah which is a sandwich of blue stone and brick, with Italian and German touches and a splendid dovecote at the back, built for Mr William Gordon Gordon, a captain of commerce.

You can discover many of these polyglot delights, this interesting juxtaposition of all sorts of building, just by walking around. There is a word for it, SHARAWAGGI, describing the vibrations when you get a new building beside an old one and the pleasant sensations their contrast gives. It is all accessible — pedestrians can get about in Port of Spain and the sights can easily be discovered and absorbed.

North of the town, when you would expect the hills, suddenly you hit the Savannah, that blessed fortuitous acreage! A glorious open space of two hundred acres. An expanse of grass, with a judicious distribution of beautiful trees on the periphery: royal palms, cannonball tress, samaans, pouis yellow and pink, flamboyants, African tulips and one or two I don't know, dotting the Savannah in perfect harmony. We must remember the Peschier family who sold us their sugar estate so that we can now enjoy it. Beyond it lie the botanical gardens, the zoo, the Governor General's house, Queen's Hall, the Hilton Hotel and free hills.

Then you should tour the suburbs for sudden surprises — churches, or maybe a mosque. So many styles of architecture side by side, what is the word for it again? SHARAWAGGI? Then into the valleys and more little houses. The towns, Arima, San Fernando, Sangre Grande and the great sounding names of these parts, Tunapuna, Carapichaima, Moruga, Guayaguayare, perhaps the only active remaining memory of the Arawaks and Caribs.

But returning to Port of Spain the town is busy, never sleeping, colourful, vibrant, untidy, complicated. The buildings are like worn clothes, patched, shabby, changed rapidly and re-styled. Let us ask how it all began. Who really started it? The Spaniards. Yes, but they did not leave much: the oval window and the façade and courtyard in the old Cabildo on Sackville Street, and precious little else. According to V.S. Naipaul, the Spaniards in St Joseph lived in Amerindian huts, and the bush has reclaimed them. In Trinidad the bush soon reclaims the wood which it so ungraciously yields to the axe for building purposes. We live and we die, and it seems in Trinidad that we cut timber and if we are not

Heading for the future.

careful it is claimed back by nature before the end of one man's life span, attacked by termites and the weather, fungus and damp heat. Grudgingly given and rapidly reclaimed. Vehicles last the same length of time comparatively, if you work it out. Buildings here mature and die quickly by comparison with those in temperate countries which, after all, still provide our yardstick. Growth and decay. Erection and demolition. Great tropical upflowering at an almost unreasonable speed, and then decay. The equalizing and the opposite elemental reaction.

However, we are not supposed to notice this. It is unseemly for visitors to observe these grim facts, so let us look at the styles. Under the English Governor Picton the French built their great estate houses in the universal grand colonial style. Functional and well designed, these houses adapted themselves to the country with high rooms, high steep gable roofs, slates, white fretwork boarding. They made use of the shipwrights' skills. Built of pitchpine and local woods such as mora and mahogany and protected against termites by arsenic, they were ideal. Cool, lofty, and dry. They were crowned with heavy turned finials and there were cast iron crestings to secure the roof. Wood and plaster walls, fretted fanlights, yellow-shuttered louvred doors and side lights — and that abomination, the English sash window. Baskets of ferns between decorated posts with fretted brackets and serrated bargeboarding. So that by the time the light and air got through to the occupants it was so baffled that the sun had long since been filtered out and the rain separated from the breeze.

The style, conceived in the eighteenth century, blossomed in the nineteenth into a Victorian *tour de force*. Raised nearly ten feet above the ground on piers and approached by graceful steps, the sugary soaring decorated dwellings dominated the landscape. The intricacies of light and shadow out-classed the flickering forest itself, and the oil lamps at night presented a succession of magnificent decorative designs for people outside looking in, an effect never to be repeated after the coming of the unblinking blandness of electric light.

Top: Cricket in the road. The interruption caused by traffic is tolerated graciously.
Bottom: Indian sweetmeats on a roadside stall.

Later, when the population of Port of Spain increased and after the great fire at the turn of the century, the town was rebuilt. The downtown stores, one against the other, had great stone firewalls built every fifty feet, rising above the adjoining roofs. The store-fronts blossomed with beautiful decorated iron balconies, graciously protecting the pedestrian underneath from the fierce sun and sudden showers. Protected from the street by slender iron posts on the pavement edge, the pedestrian could feel both safe and at ease.

Like the earlier estate houses, the design and construction of downtown Port of Spain was good. In fact too good. So good that the merchants were able to operate without doing any repairs at all. The buildings certainly held together for a long time, after seventy-five years they are now collapsing from a colossal neglect. Chosen mainly from catalogues of Scottish ironworks in Glasgow, the balconies derived in design from France and other sources. A choice of styles was available from English Georgian to late Louis XV. The balconies remain a source of delight to those who care to look at them. A few are still in place.

This turn-of-the-century flowering brought into being the suburban house as well. I am thinking especially of areas such as Woodbrook and Newtown. Delicate, fretted, feminine and entirely delightful, gabled, slated roofs, turretted galleries, *portes-cochère*, steep steps, iron gates, tall gate posts, iron railings, crotons, Lebanese grapevines, baskets of ferns, curtains, enamelled number plates, white on blue, and the wood fretwork different on each house.

Those of them spared by termites are now being spoilt by electric wiring. Crawling like the termites, leaving similar erratic and lumpy tracks, the cable makes its way into hot voids, possibly to ignite when the insulation fails. And the air conditioning units now being installed vibrate like road drills, shaking the sunken joints of the old bones of the houses, which seem about to expire.

While these suburban houses were going up, the grandees were building a series of extraordinary mansions in Port of Spain, on the west side of the Savannah, here christened The Magnificent Seven. They are seven large houses in a row, as grand, unified and complete as any group of eighteenth-century terraced houses, yet as flamboyant and daring as any Trinidadian would wish.

Starting from the north we begin with a German Scottish Baronial mansion of forbidding and permanent aspect known as Stollmeyer's Castle. Magnificently built, using difficult materials, it is a triumph of good construction and bizarre architecture. The hard stone-work is beautifully cut square and dressed to fit all the slopes, which meant a lot of selection and hacking. This battle resulted in a tight, pale, brittle building, dry and laconic, sombre and tense. It is Scottish in its narrow verticality — French influenced — and no doubt German in intent. Under the tropical sun it is difficult to say which style dominates.

The second of The Magnificient Seven is the Prime Minister's office, Whitehall. A white wedding cake of a building which has a most unusual feature for Trinidad — a parapet to hide the roof. It presents a regular but undulating façade best described as Corsican Moorish; in contrast to Stollmeyer's Castle it is tactile, inviting and seductive. Surrounded by a white wall of appropriate design it is set off perfectly by a huge dark samaan tree, parasol-like, and it is quite different from number three, the Roman Catholic Archbishop's palace which is serious and Romanesque Irish. The palace was recently repainted in killing colours, the ponderousness has been accentuated and the cumbersome mediaeval arches, always solid and dogmatic, now produce a sombre and humourless appearance. But this need not be so; the open arcading is Italian in feeling and the building could be made to come to life.

Again in contrast, the next palace, number four, is a fantastic French Baroque Colonial. It is breathtaking, and has to be seen to be believed. A series of cupolas and domes compose a sky-line which would be a credit to a French *château*. Complicated and self-opinionated, the roof caps a meandering building surrounded by high roof galleries. Obviously built for pleasure, it declares itself and has all the humour and *joie de vivre* the Romanesque-via-Ireland palace next to it lacks. Originally the Ambard residence and now known as Roodals Palace, it is a queen of architecture.

Five and six — six being the Anglican Bishop's official residence — are typically grand town houses, have iron fretwork, a pleasant *porte-cochère* and a refined setting.

The seventh, to round off the bunch, is Queen's Royal College, the locally famous boys' school, in German Renaissance style — if you please — with royal palms in front, complete with lighted clock-tower and chiming clock.

This, then, is The Magnificent Seven. All different, a real mixture you might say of Indian, French, English, Corsican, Moorish, Scottish, Italian, Romanesque and German design; heaven knows what the exact aesthetic intention of the builders was. Indeed we need no longer care. The history of The Magnificent Seven is enigmatic and derivative. The circumstances of the conception of each house are hidden in the past of the particular family which built it, and can interest only that family and historians. The history of these houses is without national significance. For example the Archbishop's Palace is Romanesque of a kind — but it is so far removed from eleventh-century France that we need not examine too closely the complicated circumstances which gave rise to it and how the movement survived and was revived and transplanted.

The Magnificent Seven are well set in a superb relationship to the Savannah. They can be seen and examined from all angles, and trees and hills seem to be arranged to flatter them. Larger than life, bold, daring, singular, they sing out the individualism characteristic of the country. Flamboyant and loud, yet heavily disciplined in their corporate setting, like a carnival band on the road — not just on any road, on The Road.

The maturing national consciousness herewith claims them as a part of ourselves, our country. Welcome! Can you not see them coming as Queens — all those of you who know Trinidad Carnival? Each a queen facing the Savannah, with her supporters (the stables) at the back and her band (the houses) behind her down Hayes Street. Proud into the wind the pennants fly as the permanent exhibition stands there for all to see. The nation can point to The Magnificent Seven as a true expression of the people, a souvenir to look at and photograph.

In the days when the grand houses were being built the ordinary people generally lived in *ajoupas* with *t'mite* roofs. Put up in a day, cool, practical and usually on the best sites near the tops of hills, because the motor cars of the rich were not yet powerful enough to climb up to lay claim to them. They used to be built, these ajoupa houses, with branches or young trees an inch in diameter. These saplings, or round wood as they were called, were about seven feet long, and provided the framework for the dwelling. At the corners or eaves the round wood would be tied by liane vines or string if handy. Further uprights would be put in to reduce the space between them. The next stage is to weave in and out of these, behind and in front of the round wood. The bamboo springs into place, making any other support unnecessary. There is no modern equivalent in building to this tension spring.

This horizontal weave is then plastered with clay, which seals the wall and finishes it off. The roof is framed and secured and thatched with bound bundles of grasses, or shingled with carat or timite fronds, or leaves.

No nails are used. Three men could easily put up a house like this in a day — or, with a little help from his friends, one man in one day. The house is cool and dry and clay is banked up around it to keep out flood water. The eaves hang low over the slit windows so that no rain or sun penetrates the openings. Nowadays small houses are usually built of wood, with some concrete blocks as a base, and galvanized iron or imported pitchpine for the roof.

With the rise of the new middle class there has been a gradual emergence of suburban houses in Diego Martin and elsewhere. Called by the writer the Diego Martin style, it has coloured split concrete walls, pipe columns, heavy cantilevers, lots of colours, varnished cedar ceilings, shedded galvanized iron roofs, iron burglar bars, grass lawns, fancy walls and a loud stereo epitomizing the style of Trinidadians today. As bold-faced as The Magnificent Seven, the new houses of Trinidad sparkle with exuberance. Luxurious in one sense, broad, wide and large, they vibrate with the sound of music and children, outdo their neighbours and are shamelessly alive. And after all what more does one really want?

Tobago is so different, another place. Although wired up to Trinidad, Tobago still remains rural, small scale, serene. Houses, little houses, are parked by the road like cars. They grew after emancipation, when Tobagonians left the plantations and planted these little cottages on curves in the road in Goodwood, Roxborough and Moriah. Architecture is not strong in Tobago — how unfortunate that this chapter is on architecture. Architecture is too precise — too European a word for what we are talking about, and too brittle. Tobago has atmosphere. A special something. The architecture of atmosphere; and in Tobago the architect should design silhouettes and be less technologically inclined.

The views are there for pedestrians, not motorists. Driving, the road swings too suddenly round curves and the hills pass too swiftly behind the houses. The car annihilates space, eating it, telescoping it like a speeded-up movie; and this in spite of the speed limit of 30 mph throughout the island (which hasn't many stretches of road straight enough to allow the attainment of this limit).

The buildings are mostly smaller than in Trinidad with smaller eaves — the old hurricane scares clipped back the eaves a bit and made the buildings tighter, like in Barbados — wood closeboarding with fretwork gables, and louvred windows. The small houses with high hipped roofs — galvanized again after the last hurricane — rest their front on the road with the back of the house often hanging propped over a precipice twenty-five feet below. Houses blown off their supports by hurricanes remain lower on the adjoining ground, with stone steps leading nowhere.

Scarborough, the capital, follows this style. A beautiful little town. The individual buildings are nothing but the town as a whole is a treasure. The wonderful Court House was one of the most superb examples of Georgian architecture in the West Indies. I say 'was' because the entrance, the best part of it, was demolished eighteen years ago. It should be rebuilt, it would not cost much. The front could be put back for sixty thousand dollars.

Government House looks odd. The Governor started to build a two-storey residence but was reprimanded because his status, based on the square miles under his governorship, only allowed for a single storey. A roof was hastily stuck on the half-finished building. Reported to be haunted, the spaces echo mysteriously with inexplicable sounds. The fact that a roof instead of an upper floor was put on Government House typifies the unsatisfactory, unfinished situation that buildings and architecture get themselves into in Tobago. Unfinished. As nature treats the trees, so the buildings of Tobago have been truncated by weather or circumstance. The old sugar mills are converted to houses, the new clinging to the old. This 'organic' or accidental architecture is saturated with mystery, charm and atmosphere, and after all, even in Europe these things are now being recognized as most important — don't you agree?

Artists and Craftsmen

M. P. Alladin

The art experience in Trinidad and Tobago is substantially the same as that of any other tropical colony or territory which became independent after long rule by a European country. From the point of view of sophistication, the accepted form or type of art expression is Europeanized, as are the materials and concepts employed in its production. This form, in art and life, is considered as being superior, desirable, right and proper. The trained artists of the country have all been schooled in Europe or Canada or the United States.

There also exists a vast amount of art production at the 'folk' level, which is worthy of consideration. These folk arts are preponderantly of African and East Indian origin. The popular arts are American-influenced.

In this article the term 'art' is used to mean painting, drawing and sculpture.

The first original art works which came to Trinidad and Tobago centuries ago were paintings on canvas brought in as symbols of 'culture' by government officials and businessmen who had travelled abroad on home-leave. These paintings were portraits of their relatives or depictions of their homeland, rendered in a true-to-life manner (this practice is carried on even today by local senior government officials). The children of Europeans were normally sent to complete their education in the parents' motherland and several took drawing courses.

The first original art works produced in Trinidad were small drawings of local landscapes done in pencil and ink-and-wash by holidaying relatives of officials and businessmen, and sometimes by members of the navy or army serving here for short periods. These pictures highlighted buildings, vegetation and seascapes, and are still being discovered today in the collection of descendants of those long-gone artists or their friends.

The first important, genuine Trinidadian artist was Jean Michel Cazabon. Born in Port of Spain in 1813 of French parents, he was sent to study medicine in France. Cazabon became so interested in painting that he gave up medical studies and trained as an artist. He returned to the West Indies to teach art in Martinique and subsequently in Trinidad, where he soon began to spend all his time attempting to earn a living from his paintings. He executed numerous water-colour landscapes in a highly realistic style. Many of his drawings of local scenes were reproduced in two series of lithographs in Paris, the cost being borne by local subscribers from the upper classes. It is due largely to Cazabon's pictures that we can still get a glimpse of how things looked in and around Port of Spain and many other parts of Trinidad about a century ago.

It was many years after Cazabon before any special attention was again focussed upon art. However, Mr Philip John, a Trinidadian and a pupil of Cazabon, held the post of Government Art Teacher for many years, and after the end of World War One, in 1918, Mr Thomas Spencer, an English master, was appointed to teach drawing, at the leading secondary school (Queen's Royal College) and the small teachers' training college located in the precincts of Tranquillity Government School. His emphasis was upon realistic draughtsmanship. His influence is still evident today when many ex-teachers and dear old ladies continue to display precisely rendered, though now faded, oils of roses and lilies and Scottish highland scenes. Furthermore, the educated members of the older generation still consider that type of painting as being best of all.

In the thirties, the arts as a whole experienced a strong shot in the arm when creative writers like Alfred Mendes, Albert Gomes, Arnold Thomasos, Ralph Vignale and pamphleteer Jean de Boissiere, and artists like Hugh Stollmeyer and Amy Leong Pang, made themselves felt with meaningful work which seemed at that time to be revolutionary. Stollmeyer, who now lives and works partly in the United States and partly at home, has remained a distinguished Trinidad artist. Leong Pang is still a black-and-white artist of talent. But art, in the intellectual sense, was still a rare commodity indulged in by a handful of the upper classes.

At the beginning of World War Two, British and American servicemen came to Trinidad. Among them were a few musicians and painters who practised their art side by side, so to speak, with a few local artists. More importance was placed upon the environment as the source of subject matter for pictures. Many foreign officers acquired paintings and a few Trinidad professionals and businessmen started doing the same — for one thing, more money was circulating in those war days. However, the techniques and the colour schemes used in the pictures were conventional European e.g. it was accepted that every painting should have 'grey' as a compulsory ingredient and any deviation from this rule generally exposed an artist to adverse criticism by the *cognoscenti*. While a few artists executed original work and looked at the environment with greater interest, many still copied post-card and magazine reproductions.

By 1943, artists like Mildred Faulkner, Sybil Atteck and Alice Pashley were talking of starting an Art Group. Among others, Albert Gomes, Andrew Carr and Amy Leong Pang joined the movement. The Trinidad Art Society was born. By 1944, the annual November Exhibition, the most important artistic event for many years, was established. Though sometimes unjustifiably accused of catering for the upper classes only, the Art Society has performed a major task in providing opportunities for young artists to develop and show their work. After some lean years the Society is beginning to revive its activities. In its heyday it sponsored exhibitions, lectures and classes throughout the year.

Before the Art Society came into existence the Teachers' Economic and Cultural Association staged annual Arts and Crafts Exhibitions at the Royal Victoria Institute, thereby creating interest in this field among teachers. The Agricultural Society in their exhibitions held on a county or national basis had, for years, provided for the display of art work for competitive purposes. Many amateur artists participated in these shows.

The British Council had, by now, set up an office in Port of Spain and began to provide positive help in the field of the arts. It is largely due to the Council's operations in music, drama and art that these activities became, to a certain degree, popular and institutionalized. They provided books, periodicals, recordings, meeting rooms and studios and even financial assistance, e.g. for the Art Society. Best of all, perhaps, they awarded scholarships and bursaries in the arts, tenable in Britain, to Trinidadians who showed talent and interest and who had had some local training in the field. While a certain number of scholars remained abroad, most returned and are still the most sound and dependable arts organizers in the country.

At the beginning of 1949 the writer of this article, the first British Council Art Scholar, was appointed to the staff of the Government Training College for Teachers to lecture in Art and Art Education and to operate in the field on a peripatetic basis throughout Trinidad and Tobago. For a dozen years thereafter he was responsible for lecturing at four teachers' colleges, for visiting schools to advise on art education, and for conducting in-service courses for teachers. He founded the Art Teachers Association in 1950 with, subsequently, eight groups throughout the two islands, and conducted free weekly classes in art for selected gifted school-students and 'amateur' artists. Materials were supplied free by the British Council. These round-the-country, round-the-year efforts at teaching, demonstrating, organizing of exhibitions and picture loan schemes, and the distribution of art materials etc, facilitated participation in and understanding of art in the widest sense. In 1958, another officer was appointed to assist in developing these activities and in 1963 still another. In 1965 the writer was appointed Director of Culture to work at the development of all the arts, including visual arts.

The sort of foundation then laid through teachers and rural art groups included liberation of the arts from overseas influences as far as expression, experiences and choice of subject matter went. Efforts were made to experiment with materials from the surroundings. The understanding that Art and Craft were, in reality, but two sides of the same coin was at last beginning to be established. Technical achievement and good craftsmanship were tied up with good design and with originality and individuality of expression.

Most of the leading present-day artists evolved out of this programme; and it is important to note that a new type of artist has now appeared, namely, the artist-art educator who has learnt and practised and taught many related skills. He is a new type of person who is increasingly appearing on the international scene.

At the moment, while art has not as yet become a very general activity in Trinidad and Tobago, we are certainly heading in that direction. A far greater number of people are aware of art, and many more creative artists have come into existence than would otherwise have been the case. In other words, this is now a much more art-conscious land.

The present Government has encouraged participation in art through the Department of Culture which recommended increased circulation of local art works in rural centres annually in a Week of Arts programme. The Government has awarded scholarships; it has taken part in overseas exhibitions — e.g. since 1963, Trinidad has taken part in every one of the São Paulo Biennials; it has purchased artists' original works for use in government offices and for the National Museum and Art Gallery which came into being from the time of Independence in 1962. This institution has a permanent display as well as a current exhibition area. The permanent collection naturally consists mainly of works by the leading local artists and a few foreign works donated as official gifts to this country by other governments. In the changing exhibition area are staged some twenty displays annually, highlighting one-man shows by leading local artists, mixed shows by art groups and institutions, and also exhibitions of reproductions and originals loaned by foreign governments. Admission is free since the Museum is regarded as an Education-Research institution. It is the one place in the country where a comprehensive collection of local art of the widest variety can be viewed. In addition, the Museum houses a representative collection of carnival costumes, a display on the steelband including its development, and some very interesting folk art — wood carvings, head-dresses, dolls, decorative items and the like. There are also small sections on history, archaeology, geology and natural history.

Large and small coloured reproductions of local art are sold at a popular price at the Museum in order to encourage the purchase and use of these by as many people as possible. Printed notes accompany these reproductions. Other material distributed free includes notes on Carnival and on the folk arts in Trinidad and Tobago.

Following upon the spread of interest in art, the Extra-Mural Department of the University of the West Indies also began the organization of art courses for amateur artists in different parts of the island.

Over the years, several voluntary art groups have evolved. The Art Teachers' Association, with strong branches in Port of Spain and San Fernando, continues to develop the capabilities of its members both as creative artists and as art-craft educators. The Trinidad Art Society has continued as a group of artists. The Southern Art Society serves San Fernando and other points south. The Tobago Art Group, as its name implies, operates in that island. In almost every case these groups include members from abroad who have come to live or work in these parts and their contribution to the many successful programmes is considerable. A wide-ranging and varied set of activities benefits all members, the main project in each case being an annual art exhibition in the centre in which the group is located.

A new feature has emerged within the last few years; namely, arts and crafts shops, several of which have been running quite successfully. Some five or six of these shops represent different individual artists. Foreign art galleries have evinced interest in exhibiting the works of artists from this country and arrangements are made through individuals or groups. However, the latter project has not gone as far as it could.

The major sales of art works are made to tourists who usually prove to be pretty discriminating in their choice.

As a rule, their purchases aim at enhancing their own collection but often they acquire art works to be used as gifts for their friends at home. These buyers come principally from the United States of America but a few come from Europe and Canada as well. Invariably, the tourist gets a good selection for his outlay, although some few have expressed disappointment at being unable to see a sufficiently large number of 'primitive' works.

One problem in this connection is that while many genuinely gifted primitive painters and sculptors do exist in the country, they have little or no faith in their own work, mainly because of the artificial and pseudo-sophisticated appreciation of this type of art by leaders in the community and even by art critics. Undoubtedly meritorious work by gifted primitives, therefore, never gets to the shops and into exhibitions. Another factor is that artists do not, as a rule, produce art work consistently, more often tending to wait for some incentive like an exhibition.

Local purchasers of art are few and far between and come mainly from the professional classes. They could almost be counted on the fingers of one hand and, in a sense, may be considered as the true patrons of art in this country. Many favour individual artists whom they attempt to promote in the manner of a patron rather than an entrepreneur.

Innumerably more paintings and drawings are produced than sculpture. Several reasons for this may be adduced. They are easier to store, to display, to transport and can normally be executed in a smaller space.

At another level of sophistication, a folk-painting tradition has been established in this country. These works are executed by self-trained artists or those who have copied traditional forms of painting. In Hindu temples, or *seewalas*, on the walls and ceilings, which are usually white-washed, are depicted gods and goddesses in traditional poses, the paint used being coloured enamels. In addition, several statues of these same characters e.g. the God Rama, and the monkey-god Hanuman, are made in sculptural form out of clay or a mixture of clay and concrete, and then painted all over with enamel paints. All forms are rendered direct in a more or less conventionally semi-primitive form.

Beautiful bead head-dresses are made for dancers and Hindu bridegrooms. Coloured paper decorations are cut in the most intricate and exquisite patterns and used for decorating wedding tents or halls where celebrations are held.

Painted decorations, wire and metal work, and papier-mâché and bead work, as well as embroidery and appliqué work, all form characteristic activities in the production of elaborate carnival costumes which depict a wide range of naturalistic and fantastic characters and which are worn for two days on street parades. To the various other craft-work such as receptacles, tools, etc., are applied geometric and simple floral incised or painted decorations, according to the material used; for example skin, clay, nut, or wood. A truly wide variety of hand-crafts with or without applied designs are produced here, despite the pressures of super-salesmanship which are employed in conditioning people to use machine-made articles from abroad.

Apart from carnival costumes, another traditional product of folk craftsmanship is the *tadjah* or *hosay*, which is built and paraded on the streets twice a year — according to the Muslim calendar. It is a sort of paper temple, some twenty-odd feet high, which is made on a bamboo frame and covered with coloured tissue and glazed paper and tinsel. It is paraded for a night and a day and then thrown into the river or the sea.

At Hindu weddings, drawings are executed on the ground with coloured powder while on the walls are printed and painted various images — hands, flowers, stars, and figures — all by amateur artists.

Much activity also exists at the popular arts level. Using enamel colours, commercial artists paint huge bill-boards copying foreign pictorial styles and symbols associated with advertised commodities and the people who use them. Since all catalogue and magazine advertisements have come from countries in Europe and North America, white people are always depicted in these copies. The 'matts' for newspaper advertisement blocks have also come from abroad, hence the same type of Caucasian image predominates. The commercial artists have been influenced by this imagery and so are the public who have therefore been conditioned to seeing pictorial images in a predominantly foreign form.

Figures and objects and trees are painted on shop signs, on carts selling various foodstuffs such as snowball, bread, ice-cream, and on vans transporting or selling clothing and other wares such as pots, pans, wine, etc. Over the years quite a wide variety of subjects have been copied. On the large walls of bars and in Chinese parlours and restaurants have been painted simplified landscapes or seascapes with one or two coconut trees, one or two girls in bathing suits, green grass, yellow earth or sand, blue seas and blue or red-orange sky. The figures are usually out of proportion: girls are rendered with huge breasts and hips but tiny hands and feet while they sport front-view eyes on profile faces and each milk-white tooth in the fixed grin can easily be counted. A tree looks like a flat disc covered with innumerable round red fruit.

In painting figures, artists always used to colour them pink with blue eyes and blonde hair. When, in 1949, the writer began pointing out to teachers and young artists that they should attempt to reflect the things around them more accurately, and reminded them that most of the inhabitants of our country have dark skin and that it is possible to reproduce this colouring, he was often greeted with laughter. The first efforts of teachers at portraying their fellow citizens honestly resulted in portraits with dark skin and hair but with blue eyes. Serious artists were already portraying dark-skinned people as such, but few of them, even now, can or will capture the true form and features of their fellow citizens.

Artists have always been concerned with perspective, though often this has been limited to showing a road tapering towards the horizon. Apart from this, there was little attempt to show depth realistically. 'Shading' was often attempted but with incongruous results, except for copies of photographic portraits — mainly of screen stars and other celebrities — when highly realistic representations were achieved.

The current artistic situation in Trinidad and Tobago is that interest and participation continue apace. There are numerous amateurs, but the bulk of the work in exhibitions and art shops is produced by about thirty 'serious' painters. Artists may be divided into three categories. Firstly, the

Caribbean joy.

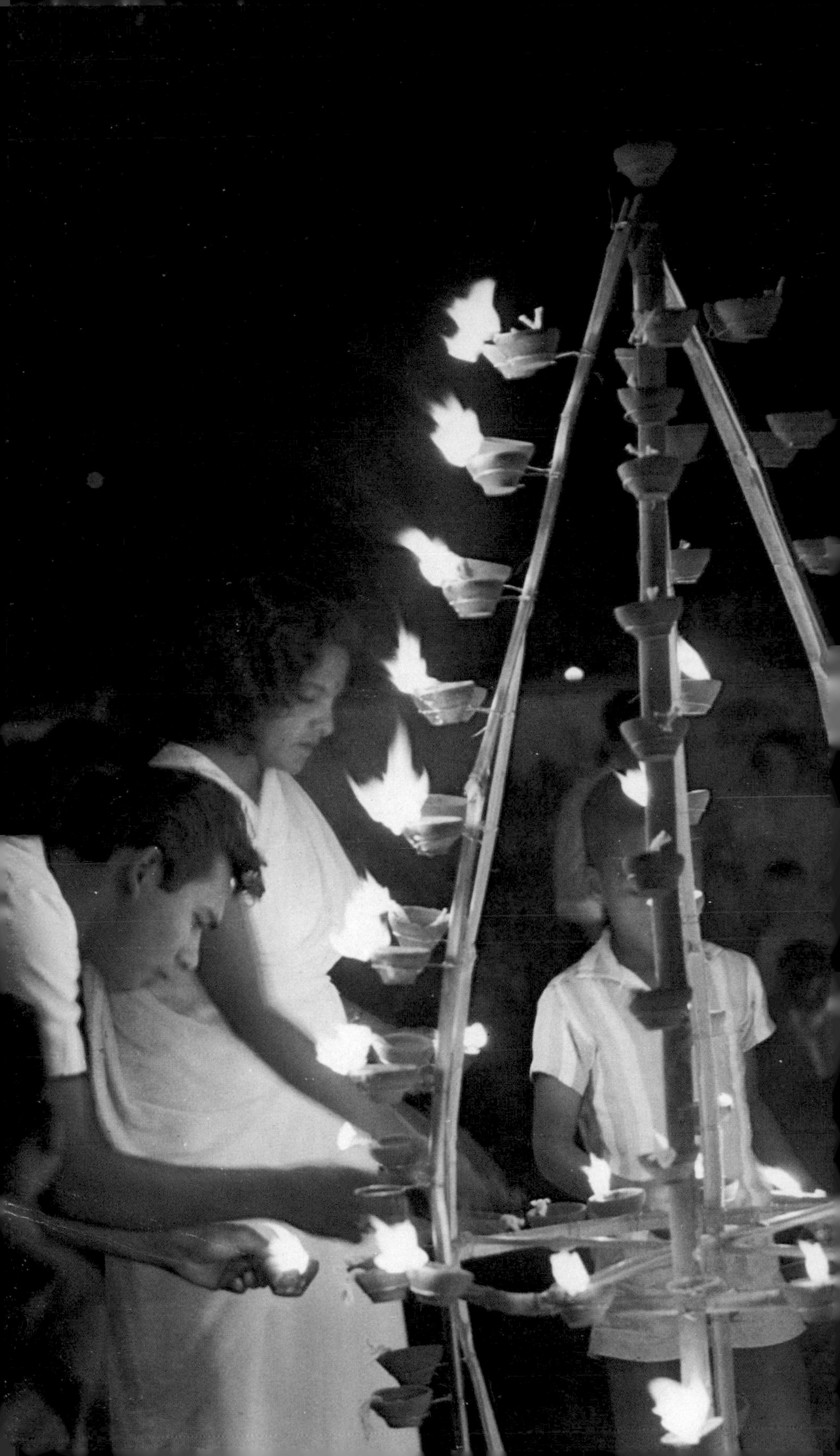

primitives whose work is done in a characteristically unsophisticated but expressive manner, often filled with emotional content. Secondly, 'amateur' artists, including commercial artists, who paint in a naturalistic manner. And, finally, a group of trained sophisticated workers whose form of expression is semi-realistic or completely non-objective. Many artists in the latter group are teachers who have received full training in the art schools of the metropolitan cities in Britain, Canada and the United States.

Art exhibitions are common. In the last year at least forty of varying size and form and degree of importance have been held throughout the country — some fifteen of these being staged at the National Museum and Art Gallery, six in rural centres by the Division of Culture, four by Art Societies and others by community groups and individual artists. Art shops also staged special shows.

A comprehensive Arts Centre has been planned by the Government and within this complex will be established display areas, a training centre (i.e. an Arts-Crafts School), research facilities, a sales section, and so on. The provision of these amenities is expected to help in the encouragement of more artists, more art works and more involvement in the arts as a whole.

While it is true that an amazing degree of philistinism and ultraconservatism exists in the art field here, it is also true that ordinary people are displaying keener interest in art and that the artist himself is increasingly concerning himself with social considerations, no matter what the nature or form of his expression.

In any country, the artist is the interpreter and the communicator and the summating channel of the essence of the culture or 'civilization'. This is true of Trinidad and Tobago and while, as in other societies and institutions, there exist a few parasites in the field of the arts, there is a genuine forward movement in the volume, quality and authenticity of the art produced by native artists.

A good example of an artist who translated national interests and verbal imagery into visual terms with meaningful results is Alfred Codallo who died in 1970. Raconteur, amateur musician and folk-lorist, he gave visible form in colour

The Hindu celebration of Diwali.

and black and white to leading characters from the country's legends as well as genre scenes depicting the life of the people in times past.

The prospect for the arts continues to be good and there can be no question that, in the years to come, Trinidad and Tobago will make a much more profound impact on the international art world.

Growing up in Tobago

E. M. Roach

Wherever you are in Tobago, turn right, turn left, the narrow rolling roads take you back to Scarborough, our only town, more village than town, crouched under historic Fort George, once bristling with King's cannon and redcoat soldiers, it guarded the town's sea entrance, Rockly Bay, from marauding pirates and hostile men-of-war. Looking out over the Atlantic, the Fort served as a landmark for incoming slavers, sugar brigantines and men-of-war sailing in on the trade winds, and from it the soldiers kept watch over half the island's plantations in the bitter-sweet days of sugar slavery.

Our vista is ocean, the Atlantic on one side, the Caribbean Sea on the other. Southward, the misty hump of Trinidad's Northern Range is seen from our own hilltops on clear days and Grenada lies further off just out of sight to the northward. Absconding slaves learnt soon enough that there was no refuge in wandering off into the bush or hiding in a town of three streets, on an island twenty-six miles long and eight miles at its widest, a mere 114 square miles altogether. In that dimension, everything is pitched in the minor key, men's hopes and ambitions, the latifundia, the villages and hamlets nestling on both sides of the Central Range, all sitting on the sea's edge, their population a mere 30,000.

In my youth it was a casual holiday weekend hike to go seeing all our villages sheltering from the sun under their dooryard trees, lulled to somnolence by trade winds and tidal rhythms. Their names — Roxborough, Glamorgan, Charlotteville, Plymouth, Culloden, Pembroke — a reflection of history, a remembrance of things past. I found the whole island an extension of my own organic pioneering village in which kinship and sustenance extended from one tree-shaded dooryard to the other, and the slow heavy rhythms of my private community were the island's rhythms, were those of a folk cut off and castaway like Crusoe himself on his own green island in the sun. If that fiction were fact then we might all be Friday's progeny.

My private cocoon, Mount Pleasant, was a sprawling bushy compound of crude wattle or clapboard cabins with thatched or tin roofs, shabby and mean like ourselves in our barefoot leeching to the earth. In later years it seemed to me that in my boyhood we were clinging to life by the skin of our teeth and did not realise our hardship because we knew nothing else. We grubbed the clay and stony soil for sustenance. In good seasons the crops grew green and flourished, but in droughts we 'caught hell', 'boiled bush' and drank 'hot water tea'. To help us, nature provided land crabs living in holes in the ground, manicous and iguanas (larger lizards) which we hunted in the bush. Then again, landless men could earn small wages — thirty-six cents per day on the neighbouring coconut estates. Some of that money went back to the estate owner for land rents for provision gardens.

In memory now the village's dooryard fruit trees — mango, genip, soursop, sugar apple, plum and citrus — seem to have been generally considered common property. I used to feel free to enter any dooryard and ask for some of whatever was ripe on the trees or fallen to the ground. The only price demanded was the currency of respect. The elders insisted on this and it seemed some precious intangible from person to person, family to family, binding us all together, to the mulatto schoolmaster with his terrible leather strap, to the parson living near the church on the hill and to the estate owners farther off.

To forget to greet an older person respectfully was to earn condemnation. There was such a droll dignity about our barefoot respectability.

'Hi boy, ent you is Brer Ezekiel son?' a man would ask me on the village road though he knew the answer well.

'Yes sir,' I would murmur trying to get away.

'Wait right there, boy. What happen to you at all? You lossing you manners or something?'

'No sir.'

'Well then, how you passing people straight on the road so? You blind? You modder ent learn you to tell people a decent howdy?'

'Yes sir.'

'Arright, go where you going boy. But don't forget you' manners next time, you hear me?'

'Yes sir.'

If my parents were told of that misdemeanour I would hear a lot about it later on. 'But how you could meet big people in the road and don't tell them howdy?' my mother would remonstrate. 'You mean after all I teaching you, and you going to school every day and you not a dunce, everybody know that, you getting on so? All you young generation, yes!'

So, down the road, as we said in the village, I had to pass the time of day with everybody — Coz Pheobe and Coz Tartie, Brer Feddie Archie, Mr Baas Lapiste, the blacksmith, Nen Velena, my godmother, going out to jovial, good-hearted Uncle Sam at the other end of the village and Nen Louisa, taciturn, unsmiling, soured with the world.

I think this excessive deference to the elders derived from the servile attitude forced on the slaves by the masters which a century of freedom could not remove. It was passed on as natural behaviour and the proper mode of conduct from one generation to another. You could not drop the folk titles of respect or somebody might drop a lash across your back.

In Scarborough where my father sent me to our only and just started high school with the solemn instruction to tip my cap to every lady or gentleman I met in the street, I discovered the world was not so homely, charitable or well-ordered as the village. Things which cost nothing in the village had a commercial value in the little market square stuck in the town's centre. And that new world of clustered houses was a motley melange of whites, blacks, Chinese, Syrians, mulattoes and other half breeds who all regarded me as a 'country bookie', 'nègre jardin' and introduced me to an inferiority complex.

Later still I was to learn that I had spent my childhood in a period of history known as the depression, the gulf between two wars; and how poor were the poor of the world then! I also discovered what it was to be born in the British Caribbean at that particular moment of history when the islands were hovering in the half dawn of post-slave feudalism, between the great gloom of slavery and entry into the modern world. My father's generation were people whose parents had been slaves and the old men and women of my boyhood were like figures in bas-relief, half-emerged from the heavy clay of our tragic past. I have always wished I were a sculptor to preserve some of those patient work-worn faces. They are not seen again. Society has shifted to another plane. Folk do not wrestle with the earth with their bare hands for sustenance as they did. The faces are now cast in a softer, more human mould.

Stuck like a wart on the eastern end of the village our homestead was almost self-sufficient in food, but we were joined to the village by a dirt track our bare feet tramped out and by tough earthy tendons of kinship and fellowship. The plough was not known to us and apparently was never used on the slave sugar plantations. When my father wanted to put a field under corn (maize) pigeon peas, cassava (manioc) or sweet potatoes he called on five or six of his friends to lend him hand-labour*. Together they hacked down the shrub with cutlasses. After a few days we raked the dried saplings into heaps (boucans) and set fire to them of an evening. Next day the burnt field was a quilt of fire-blackened, ash-strewn patches. On the edge of the rainy season the friends would come to 'lend-hand' again. They set on the earth with great-bladed hoes, chopping up rows of mounds across the field for sweet potatoes or cutting rows of twin holes for corn and pigeon peas which always went together as a crop.

These men were the cronies with whom my father shared a hog at Christmas time. They gathered in the dooryard on Christmas Eve, holiday easy out of their great labourings, their heavy voices and laughter droning in the early sunlight. They strung the squealing hog head down from the plum tree

* Called 'lend-hand' in Tobago and 'gayap' in Trinidad, it is a rural community system by which friends and neighbours give each other voluntary assistance on their land holdings.

behind the kitchen which served the threefold purpose of storehouse for our dried grain and root crops, a woodfire cooking place and an eating room. They slit the hog's throat with a cutlass and, by mid-morning the carcass would be white-clean and quartered among them and they would be gone, each carrying the precious Christmas meat wrapped in green plantain leaves.

Though I am now as old as they were I still remember those men. After four decades out of the womb of the village I can still see them, strong and slow-moving, carrying their hoes on their shoulders into the field and methodically thumping the earth, compelling her to yield them sustenance. Rivers of sweat poured from them under our fierce sun. At midday they would sit in the shade of a tree where I fetched them food and drink my mother prepared. They would eat and talk in their slow heavy way our village patois, a thick clayey African-English dialect.

Delightful to remember too that one of them was the official umpire to our village cricket team. This was a time when every team 'walked' with its own umpire making the team officially twelve. If by some mischance you went to play an away-match without your twelfth man you went foredoomed to defeat since his arbitrary decisions were part of the team's stock-in-trade.

So Brer Angas, tall and massive, was our umpire, a pillar of support to our side when 'things were tight'. If we were batting and runs were short no one would expect him to give one of us out leg before wicket. To the most just and clamorous appeal he would mutter 'good play, good play' with a straight face, and the game went on. If our opponents were batting and going guns he would cut them down with a raised finger even without an appeal. His great size and his ability as a boisman (stickfighter) made him immune from physical attack. When my father and the rest twitted him about his umpiring he would say, 'Man, I playing me game, yes! I can't stand up there and see the boys loss easy so.'

Oh, our village cricket on a hoed-off dirt pitch in a rough pasture was a fierce partisan game of fast straight bowling and hefty hitting. The men with keenest eyes and strongest and straightest arms were the only heroes we ever had.

On the days they failed us we perished miserably and our old captain could be heard crying his doleful lament, 'Ah Select, water in me eye, water in me eye.' On the days of our triumphs we went home singing our victory ditty,

'If you follow Select boys
You will get fever
And the fever will never recover.'

It was a rough school for a boy to learn the game in, but it stood me in good stead in the school in town; it gave me status among the town lads. Later on I carried on into one of the island's senior teams where I learnt more of the refinements and subtleties of the game. Cricket was part of the fabric of my growing up, part of the web of my young life.

The god of the poor simple peasantry of the earth dwelt among us in our rough cabined dooryards under the trees, in our hard labourings, in the helping hand we extended each other in need and by which the old and the sick were nurtured. There was no state charity in my boyhood. The work-worn old men and women lived on aid from their friends and kinfolk or turned their faces to the wall and willed themselves to death. My mother was our dispenser of family charity, her children the conveyors. She would send us out with gifts of food — a meal, milk, eggs or home-baked bread — to the old and ill. Our instructions were to say that she sent 'howdy' and to find out how the recipient for whom she was praying was 'feeling'.

If my mother's charity was large her faith was absolute. Every night, with the slow mumbling and finger tracing of the barely literate, she read the black family bible which carried on the flyleaf, written in my father's careful sloping hand, the record of her marriage and her giving birth. She thumbed it through from Genesis to Revelation though only her God alone knows what she could make of that mass of material whose full meaning I began to grasp much later on from the writings of biblical scholars and theologians. She knew whatever happened was 'Gord will'. He punished and He blessed. He sent the rains and she offered prayers against the drought. She was in fact a familiar of the 'Lord giveth and the Lord taketh away', and 'Blessed be the name of the Lord', her Sunday Morning and Evensong and Holy Communion and my reluctant Sunday school goings. God sent the hurricane to punish us because the world was waxing grossly in iniquity. 'The world today worse than Sodom and Gomorrah I tell you. Gord hand heavy on us this day, but in his mercy he will spare the righteous,' she said.

We trooped up the hill in our Sunday clothes, picking our way in shoes unworn all week, over the loose stones of the road to the church among the tamarind trees. We went up also for the rites of baptism, marriage and burial, leaving our dead there in the field sloping down to the village road after much sorrowful hymn-singing and unrestrained weeping by the women folk.

But we accompanied each formal ritual of the Church of England with a dooryard festival of our own devising. In homely antics we summoned the dimly remembered pagan deities of Africa to revisit us before and after we carried out the edicts of the God of Israel.

A fetish of red and black beads was strung round the new-born baby's neck to ward off 'maljo' (*mals yeux*) evil eyes. On the Sunday of its baptism festivities were held in the dooryard to which each guest fetched the child a silver coin for prosperity in its life.

But a christening was really a minor social event, an intimate family affair compared with a marriage or a death. Weddings and funerals were great communal occasions. The wedding embraced the whole village community and netted kinfolk and friends farther afield. No formal invitations were issued. The message went round by word of mouth and people would turn up to clean up the wedding dooryard and build a great tent of green bamboo poles and coconut fronds, to kill the pigs and chickens and cook the masses of 'ground provisions' (root crops) they fetched as wedding gifts. They had nothing else to give.

Festivities began in the dooryard on the evening before the wedding day. Drummers and fiddlers entered to make the music for the wedding dance. The older women held up their long skirts to trip the unshod toe in the dust in bélé, reel, jig, lancers and quadrille. The old men thumped the goat-skin drums in half remembered African rhythms and scraped their fiddles lustily. All night long fires burned in the dooryard to warm the goatskin drums; the drummers warmed themselves on rum, the dancers on rhythm and the trees regarded our stolid peasant jollity.

Come midnight, someone, a young girl most likely, overcome by the drums, the frenzy of her own motion and probably one unaccustomed rum too many, would fall unconscious in the dancing circle muttering incoherences which some interpreted as prophecies of the couple's future life together. Often the act was feigned and the prophecy envious or malicious gossip. But the prophetess was said to be in the power of or to be 'ridden' by the spirit of some dead ancestor. In the folk idiom we declared 'she ride, she ride' while she blessed or doomed the marriage with her half comprehensible mutterings.

Next noon the drummers and fiddlers played the couple from the churchyard into the dooryard and there was a whole afternoon's feasting and speechmaking for the gaily dressed guests in the flower-hung tent and general merriment for all in the dooryard. The toastmaster, the village orator whose services were sought through several villages, a man of random flowery phrases that sent his audience into raptures, ruled the order of the compliments which nearly every man present wanted to pay. He hogged the speaking time and commanded most of the plaudits, and as the toasts built up, the more reckless and meaningless was his verbiage. Beyond the contrivance of words, we ate hugely, cut the bridal cake and drank ginger beer, sorrel and home-made wines and were warm together in our communal happiness.

Funeral invitations or notices were not sent out by private word of mouth. They were publicly broadcast in our own and neighbouring villages by criers sent round to deliver the 'dead message'. Two or three men would go out walking together in the night shouting as they went, 'Who hear tell other one, Simon Quarkoo dead oh.' Over and over went their cry down the village road going away into the distance.

That gloomy heraldry of night was an open invitation for everyone to go to the 'dead house' to meet the bongo dancing in progress in the dooryard, hymn singers indoors with the dead, and coffee makers busy in the kitchen. The pagan ritual of the dance on the one hand and the Christian hymns on the other surely provided our dear departed safe conduct into the unknown, whether their road went up or down. The bongo dancing, by men only, was sheer pornography. The only explanation I've ever heard for it was that it incited the audience and the participants to lust so that the dead one would soon be replaced by new lives. But that's an invitation I personally cannot credit. For in that warm green tribal compound we needed no incentive to persuade us into each other's arms. Our cabins were too small to separate our parents from us at nights and so we learnt our sex from them and from the animals. Love was so free and natural to us that afterwards in cities I was repelled by prostitution. I could not understand why people had to buy and sell what I had grown up sharing so simply and naturally.

On the morning of the funeral the village carpenters strolled into the dooryard of the dead with their tools and if necessary some of them carried a cedar board on their shoulders to make the 'corfin'. There was a lot of food cooked in the dooryard by the women for the carpenters and sympathizers who sat about chatting and occasionally singing hymns, and for the gravediggers who had gone up the hill to sink the grave in the soft dead rock of the churchyard which gave us clean dry lodgings at the last and where I should certainly like to be buried, close to my father, when the time comes*.

After we interred the dead in the late evening, the hymn singing, coffee-drinking, biscuit-eating wake was held for nine nights in the dooryard. The number nine must have held some folk significance which I have forgotten, for after a mother had given birth she was confined for nine days before she was allowed to venture out again. Did the obeah man or woman impose it? Hardly likely. They had little to do with births and funerals. It was the old village midwife, armed with only the licence of her experience, who ruled the maternity room, and the choir master the hymn-singing wakehouse.

* Eric Roach died in April 1974, and was buried not in his village churchyard but at the Anglican Cemetery, Diego Martin, in Trinidad. Eds.

I cannot remember seeing a doctor in my village when I was a boy. Afterwards I learnt there only used to be three on the island and they were certainly very hard to come by in times of sickness. The obeahman was therefore always ready to conjure up some folk medicine for the sick. Times I heard my mother say that somebody or other had been to our only hospital in Scarborough and the doctor 'could not find the person's complaint' and had sent him home to die, 'poor thing'. This was a natural breach for the obeahman to enter to prefer his art or craft. He would burn an 'eternal light' under the bed and annoint the 'poor thing', already at death's door, with his foul-smelling concoctions. He exorcised the 'evil spirit' which he claimed to have entered the sick person with the same ease he used to cast a spell on an erring lover on behalf of the unloved one. Some laughed at, while others went in awe of the doings of the obeahman. But it was difficult to know then or recall now where the laughter ended and awe began, because some of the people who dropped in to gossip with my mother about the obeah doings of others fell under her condemnation as soon as they turned their backs. 'Don't mind she,' my mother would say, 'she come here laughing "gil gil", but every week she inside the obeahman house, the two of them making their simi-dimi. And every Sunday morning she in church pious as a lamb. I tell you what, Gord have patience in truth yes. If Gord was like man, many of us would sit down inside the church like pillar of salt and can't come out.'

People dropped in casually and talk flowed easily in the dooryard. I well remember the moonlight nights I sat out listening to the old men and women, inveterate gossips or 'confounded liars' as my father called some of them. Creators and conductors of legends, they peopled the roads and woods with jumbies (ghosts), douens, papa-bois and jack-o-lanterns who led people astray in the bush, and beautiful fairy-maids who are seen only near ponds and streams. I myself saw a fairy-maid one day. I have not invented her. We were in the coconut field, my father and I, and there she was, suddenly out of nowhere, a clay brown woman gliding to the water hole from which our cattle drank. I called to my father and pointed her out, but he replied with muted warning, 'Leave her alone. Mind your business, boy.' Taciturn and spare of speech, he never afterwards told me who or what she was. But I can see her still, gliding to the pond as if moving on air. Was she the last of the Caribs in our district, or in truth the legendary fairy-maid? Someone said once that my mind created her out of the tales I'd heard, or that I'd dreamed the incident and thought it real. But ....

Just on thirteen, my father thrust me out of the warm organic cocoon of the village, not to fend for myself, but to take the six mile daily journey to the recently started high school in town. It was a journey from the past into the future, from simple tribal ignorance into the society of the world. Later I came to regard my journey as symbolic of the whole tidal movement of the Caribbean from its nineteenth-century morass of illiteracy, servitude, poverty and folk customs into the glittering, heartless, murderous menage of twentieth-century western civilization.

The school, an old wooden 'greathouse' just outside the town, was strange, challenging and exciting then, but later I came to regard it as an irony. They tried to open the heads of dim peasant boys and girls and dibble in the seeds of mathematics, Latin, French and Spanish (mercifully no Greek, though the young Barbadian head was a Greek scholar), English Literature and History, Geography and the New Testament. Names and deeds of distant dead men — Caesar, Napoleon, Marlborough, Wellington, Nelson — of campaigns, battles and sieges, sprouted and multiplied in my head, noxious as weeds. Passages of English poetry rolled off my tongue. I strutted about like Naphthali mouthing that European rubbish. I left my mother speechless with my word knowledge of the gospels as we had to learn whole passages by heart.

Although Cambridge school-certificated, we left school knowing absolutely nothing of ourselves, our country, its history and circumstance. We were adolescents lost between two worlds; one to which we belonged by birth but were educated to reject, the other we discovered in the books. We were, to coin a phrase, 'exoticized natives'. My individual luck was that I loved to read and so afterwards discovered, as adventitiously as did Columbus himself, the Caribbean, its several peoples, my own tribe particularly, its origins and the tragic history that flung us on the islands. It was this self-acquired knowledge of my own time and place and circumstance that turned me round again and taught me to bless the school and the two clerics of the English middle classes (Bishop Anstey and Archdeacon Davies) who founded it in 1925, and through us, gave our island a place in our two-island country and the world.

But this comparative maturity was reached many years after I had walked out of the school as a black British adolescent into the harsh reality of a Crown Colony which then refused my colour the inheritance for which the school had trained me.

An Englishwoman Discovers Tobago

Wenda Parkinson

It was love, love at first sight, first smell, first touch: the classic love that changes your life, beguiles you to leave home and family and leads you to some distant, enchanted island which should be alien and strange to you but instead seems more familiar and close than the green fields, pale washed skies and white faces which surrounded you as a child.

It happened when we first saw Tobago. We landed at dusk fifteen years ago in that strange hushed hour after sunset when the wind drops, the seas quieten and the steamy air clinging round your arms and legs smells of crushed grass and the dusty heat of the day. We looked at each other then and knew it was inescapable, we had come home. We stayed that time for several weeks, stretching out our holiday long after we should have returned. We explored every road and trace, clambered perilously down into deserted bays to lie blissfully spread-eagled on the warm, gritty sand. We scrambled up the stony river beds through gothic corridors of bamboos, jumped into the deep pools and slid through the unexpected waterfalls. Every new bird and insect seemed miraculous. We were like intoxicated children finding again the key to the secret garden.

We returned bemused to our familiar life, but nothing was ever quite the same again. Every year we flew back to Tobago and every year our hearts ached as we left it. Coming at last to our senses we realized that moping for a dream world was nonsensical if that dream was achievable, so eight years ago we came to a decision and emigrated to Tobago. We found land, and there we built our house. Some people say it seems more like a temple than a house.

So be it; it wasn't considered too absurd to build a temple to a woman, why not to an island?

We weren't naïve enough to think that we could uproot ourselves and move into a new life, a new country, among people who were strange to us, of a different colour and race, without altering many of our old ways, our preconceived ideas and perhaps bruising our illusions. It's a very different thing to visit than to live.

The first lesson was an old one. Every country has its own pace, it's not only impossible to alter it, it's presumptuous even to attempt it. Eight years have passed and now it seems natural to walk more slowly. If something isn't done today it's not necessarily a crime to do it tomorrow. If guests arrive half an hour, an hour late, what of it? It needn't be a waste of time to sit and 'study your mind', or even just to sit. Faulkner wisely said that 'idleness breeds all our virtues, our most bearable qualities'; well, the rocker's on the gallery, the hammock's in the shade. Doing nothing well is at its best an art.

I had expected village life in Tobago to be very different from that in Essex, England, but it's not. There are the same feuds and petty jealousies, the same banding together against the 'outsider', and here as there an 'outsider' can have been born five miles away. In Tobago the village children are more indulged, more physically caressed, the old are more loved and respected and cared for within their families; maybe that's why the old here seem to have more pride and dignity than their counterparts in Britain or in the States.

There is far more informal spontaneous house-to-house visiting here. Christmas is a joyous time of dropping by for a chat and a song, a glass of rum, sweet cakes and sorrel — a delicious drink made from the red floral parts of the West Indian Sorrel.* Every house has been cleaned and repainted, with fresh curtains fluttering at the windows. For Christmas everything has to be 'slick'.

The women share their lives, helping each other with their children, with the sick, sewing holiday clothes and doing the washing together — in the old days in the streams,

* The sorrel plant is a species of hibiscus — *Hibiscus sabdariffa* — called sorrel or roselle. Eds.

Scarlet Ibis in the Caroni Bird Sanctuary — one of Trinidad and Tobago's national birds and a sight no visitor should miss.

where they would wash even what they were wearing, all accompanied by gossip and a lot of ribald laughter. Here it would be hard to be lonely. The men, as in English pub life, go down to the 'Snackette' to play 'all fours', to brag and drink, or sit expatiating and putting the world to rights on the culverts under the street lamps. Weddings, with the days of preparation of food and clothes, have a world-wide flavour. But funerals here are very different. Wailing announces a 'dead' and news travels fast. A wake here has the brisk cheerful atmosphere of a village fête, there's plenty of drinking to comfort the bereaved, there's card playing and open-air hair-cutting, everyone brings a few dollars, a bottle, part of a goat, pig or chicken. The corpse lies in the midst of this activity to be viewed and admired as he never was in life. It's a good time for the living and the dead.

The people of Tobago are beautiful and strong, proud and independent. Forced by the past to be fatalists and stoics, they are unexpectedly tender and loving. It would be impossible to dissemble to a Tobagonian, they see past the words and winning smiles, they look at a man and they know him. If they do not like what they find they are pitiless, if they love you it is for life.

The happy, laughing faces the visitor sees are only half the truth; how could it be otherwise, the past is still here amongst us, the future not decided. They are wary and do not trust each other easily, nor do they forgive or forget.

Their humour is sharp, sophisticated, often cruel. They are natural story tellers. An anecdote is not casually delivered but is savoured with a Shakespearean turn of phrase and gesture. Their laughter can spring as easily from disaster as from wit. Here derision throws defiance in the face of tragedy and the best way to defeat death is to laugh at it.

People who don't know us ask, rather irritatingly, 'but what do you *do* in Tobago?' which is I suppose a valid question when you live an urban life. Certainly there are no art galleries, concerts or theatre, but country life has much the same pattern anywhere and there are so many things to do that there never seems time to do them all.

Some of our happiest times have been spent walking the old tracks that cross the high lands of Tobago. These old

Top: The immortelle in flower, with cocoa planted under it, as it often is. Bottom: The ruins of a sugar mill in Tobago. There are many such traces of the past buried in the forest.

roads are, I believe, unique to this island. They meet and part and lead maze-like to nowhere, but once they had an important purpose. Some were built by the French during the Napoleonic wars to haul their cannon to points of vantage; you still find traces of a rough pavé and there are battle sites, graves, abandoned cannons, badges and buttons which survive to prove those pointlessly desperate times. There's 'Dead Man's Bay', a cold grey place where the sun never seems to reach; an old man planting above it told me 'the bodies piled there on the shore and the sea was red with blood,' speaking as if he'd seen it all himself.

Many of the narrow tracks are simple sugar roads, gently graded for the oxen to carry the sugar to the factory or down to the sea to the waiting ships. The ruined hewn coral storehouses, the mill wheels, the dams and the frightful slave sweat-boxes are all still to be found, covered with creepers and ferns and now mercifully homes only for lizards. You can walk these paths into the high forest and on to the main ridge, unlikely to meet anyone else except a guilty, giggling hunter with a forbidden cocrico bird in his bag, or a stately old couple who still bother to farm the land, making their way to the high pastures where the soil is deep and rich.

Brilliantly coloured little-seen birds startle you as they flash by into the undergrowth, and huge soft moths fly blindly and aimlessly round you as you walk. Once, as we came over the top of a bare ridge we looked down into the bowl of a valley and suddenly hundreds of shrieking parrots exploded upwards like fireworks, improbable green roman candles against the orange immortelle trees.

Sometimes these paths follow a stream with neat little rustic bridges or a ford where you can dabble your feet and watch the clumsy crayfish paddling — always backwards, it seems to me — in the clear water.

It's all absurdly, lushly idyllic. Whoever would expect to see at dusk a whole valley veiled with enormous white moon-flowers, or to find a rare cultivated passion flower in the bush, miles away from any garden: a legacy of forgotten residents who once excitedly planted the seeds that arrived on the long-waited clipper, perhaps sent all those years ago by compassionate horticultural friends. Nothing remains but the flowers.

The game fishing off Tobago can, I know, be bettered in the Caymans or off the coast of Florida. But our kind of fishing is not the classy cabin cruiser kind anyway, it's to fill our stomachs and, hopefully, the deep freeze. We leave as 'day cleans' in an open pirogue with hand lines, hopefully on a day when the dolphin are running and the flying-fish spawn streams like mercury bubbles just below the oily surface. Then when you catch one dolphin the whole shoal gathers round you; they come to the side of the boat, the hooked and the free, thrashing and leaping, and suddenly the fishermen are shouting and laughing, sitting astride the fish and pinning them in the bottom of the boat, atavistic and merciless with their raised wooden clubs. Then it's all over and quiet, the butterfly colours of the dolphin quickly fade, the booby birds swoop on the boat and we make for shore to wash away the blood and salt in the fresh-water lagoons that lie behind the beaches. After the relentless sun and wind and pitching sea it's perfection to lie in the still, shaded green water. Then back to the sea to lift the pots, hoping for lobsters, young groupers or red-fish and the little grey grunts that taste so sweet.

Our boat looks like a pirate's long-boat and its ancestors must have crept in and out of these coves. There's a 'Pirates Bay' here where the old buccaneers had safe hidden mooring and could re-water their ships. Every right-thinking Tobagonian believes there is buried treasure on the island. There are many stories of doubloons spilling down the cliff face in a landslide, a mysterious boat that arrived from Scotland, of all suitable places, bearing an old marked map and a crew who only came ashore after sunset, leaving hurriedly after being seen carrying chests on board at dead of night. Treasure in tombs, in caves, beneath the tallest trees! Oh, wouldn't it be lovely!

But our boat is only a fishing boat pure and simple. Named *Fish like a Viking*, recalling a well-known calypso, it was, to ensure its success, properly christened. A boat christening is a semi-solemn occasion. It requires a godmother and father, a minister to bless the boat and to pound out the evil spirits, sweet oil, rice, money and flowers to scatter, and a bottle of wine to smash on the side. The minister preaches long, earnestly and loudly and then the boat is taken out to sea and given a good lashing with a rope to show it the way it should go. Back to shore for rum, chicken pelau and even a cake. We left our boat as night fell in the Bay, circled by candles flickering round it on the sand. All this should protect it and ensure success for those who sail in it. Sometimes a jealous rival will place a big fat toad in your boat, nets or fish pots. Then you will never catch, not until you have removed the 'blight', perhaps with a 'red lavender' wash, which you can find in the local stores — a curious potion which smells like Eau de Javel but has more sinister associations. No one around here seems to know exactly what it is, and I don't enquire too much. There are many secret rites here on this island.

Tobago has a something that is hard to define, like Kashmir, its beauty breathes out a strange mystic quality, of which some people are instantly aware — it's hard to stand on the high hills and deny that the body also has a soul. But there is another face too, a brooding one, with the evil of ancient forgotten things. When I first came here an un-wise old woman told me that the island had been cursed; it could be true, there's a precedent for a serpent in Paradise. The broken pottery and the axe-heads (here called thunder stones) of the chillingly cruel Caribs are still easily scratched from the surface of the land and standing on the black sands of King Peter's Bay as night approaches a frisson at the back of your neck makes you turn quickly towards the trees. It's not hard to believe that King Peter (the last of the Carib warriors) is still there in the shadows, watching, waiting.

Of course everyone expects the beaches of the Caribbean to be poster perfect. In Tobago they are. There is every variety of sea and sand. There's the dreamy idyll of Pigeon Point which is exactly how Tahiti ought to look and sadly does not; there are the coral-strewn, driftwood littered beaches that are ridiculously true to every escapist's dream; and there is even surprisingly sea which provides very good surfing — not of the Californian cult variety but the less daring horizontal kind.

Buccoo Reef is justly one of the well known reefs of the West Indies. Although it's well away from the shore it is possible there for even the old and the timid to discover the new dimension of the under-sea world, which the young now take for granted. For the more experienced adventurous there are many other reefs, all round Tobago, all unexploited, almost unexplored and there are fortunately several guides and teachers to take you through the critical pangs of the tanks and the deep waters.

Carnival in Trinidad is something so unique that Tobago, of course, cannot compete. We have our little carnival, but it can be nothing compared to the upsurge of talent and life that explodes in Trinidad. But we do have one or two jollifications that are really our own. The Easter goat and crab races at Buccoo are typical of an old fashioned West-Indian 'bacchanal'. It's a day for high-style dressing, drinking, eating and gambling. There are ludicrously mock-serious races with the goats' jockeys in silks and the crabs' trainers — usually spectacularly buxom ladies — dressed in military style. There's a tremendous crowd and the bustle, dust, noise and gaiety reverberates throughout the whole island.

Harvest festival in Parlatuvier is very much an island celebration too. Parlatuvier is a remote little village of candy coloured houses sprinkled round a perfect deep bay. No one seems to know the origin of the festival, it seems more important than just the ordinary harvest thanksgiving. There is, of course, a church service with flowers, fruit, cakes and bread, and all the women and children sing and parade with bouquets of flowers. But later there's rounders on the beach, maypole dancing, feasting, singing and jumping-up to the steel bands. Calypso singing-parties pass from one house to the next, tirelessly and ceaselessly, for two happy exhausting days and nights.

I have never really thought of myself as a foreigner in Tobago, and even those who do when they first come here soon fall under the spell; this is a land that opens its arms wide to you and then holds you quietly there, so that unknowingly you become a part of it, and it becomes a part of you.

I am still unhappy when I leave here and always full of unreasoning joy when I return and the aeroplane comes in to land and once more I see the thin white shore with its palm fringe, the reef and the high blue hills behind and I know that here I am, now I am content, I have come home again.

Natural History

Victor C. Quesnel

'There we saw houses and people and very fair lands, lands as beautiful and green as the gardens of Valencia in the month of March.' Thus wrote Columbus to the King and Queen of Spain in 1498, and the country he was describing was the island of Trinidad which he had recently discovered and named. The traveller to Trinidad today will probably still consider these words appropriate, even though he may never have seen the gardens of Valencia; for Trinidad is indeed a fair land, beautiful and green.

It is a green land because it falls within the humid tropics. Here, Nature's abundance manifests itself in a vast array of species rather than in a multitude of individuals of any one species. Thus the field of buttercups, the host of daffodils, the lilac haze of heather on the moors of England have no counterpart in Trinidad except where man has left his own imprint on the landscape. In the cacao-growing areas, immortelles set the hills aflame with vermilion blooms early in the dry season — but these are not native trees; they were introduced long ago as shade for the cacao plants, which were themselves introduced by the early Spanish settlers. Sometimes, on the hills that solicitously encircle the capital city of Port of Spain, the yellow poui bursts into a breathtaking display of golden blossoms. Caught in the rays of a bright morning sun as they reach out into the vibrant sky, they produce an ecstacy of delight in all but the most insensitive beholder. But though the poui is a native tree and is not at all rare, its numbers are not such as to rival Wordsworth's host of daffodils. Green is the predominant colour of the tropical landscape; now, as in Columbus's time, Trinidad is a green land.

Trinidad and Tobago are geologically and biologically part of continental South America, but because Tobago was separated from Trinidad many thousands of years before Trinidad was separated from Venezuela, the difference between Tobago and Trinidad is greater than that between Trinidad and Venezuela. Tobago resembles to some extent the Windward Islands to the north; Trinidad is hardly more than an extension of the Paria peninsula of Venezuela.

Beard, in his great work on the natural vegetation of Trinidad, divides the natural vegetation into communities grouped into two broadly different types according as their main features are determined primarily by climatic factors or by soil conditions. All the forest communities of lowlands, hills and shore are climatic formations; the various swamp communities and the savannah communities owe their peculiarities to soil conditions. Obviously, it is impossible to give even a brief survey here of all of them. Only a few highlights can be mentioned, and to some extent personal experience determines the choice, though an attempt is made to describe what may be most interesting or accessible to the visitor to the island.

Evergreen or semi-evergreen seasonal forests covered most of the lowland areas of primeval Trinidad, including the central range up to 1,000 feet and the northern range up to about 800 feet. Deciduous forest occupied much of the northwestern peninsula and the islands to the west. The vegetation one sees on the hills surrounding Port of Spain is the remnants of this formation. One of the dominant trees is the yellow poui already mentioned. Its spectacular blossoming in the dry season is a delight to the eye. Legend has it that the poui flowers three times before the rainy season, and in a general way this may be true. My observations suggest that the yellow poui flowers in response to rain after a period of drought. When the dry season is not severe the flowering is sporadic. When a intense period of drought of a month or more is broken by a spell of heavy rain all the trees seem to flower simultaneously and abundantly. Later periods of rainfall induce further bursts of flowering but these are never as spectacular as the first. A smaller and less conspicuous relative, the black poui, follows the same pattern of flowering; while throughout the dry season a more distant cousin, the bois lezard, like a pointilliste painter, sprinkles the northwestern peninsula with inconsequential yellow dots.

Other notable trees in the deciduous forests are the cypre, purpleheart, tantakayo, cedar, silk cotton, cannonball, chaconia. The first four all provide excellent timber for furniture, buildings and ornaments, the cedar being notable for its resistance to termites. Silk cotton is an enormous tree and a fine example can be seen at the corner of Belmont Circular Road and Queen's Park East. Many old trees have hollow trunks and possibly the bats that inhabit them are the tangible expression of the spirits that must be assuaged whenever a tree is cut down. The tree sheds its leaves completely at the height of the dry season and seeds embedded in a puff of cotton drift off on the season's winds to cover a wide area as they come to rest. The chaconia, the national flower, is perhaps more typical of the lower montane forests than the seasonal forests, though it occurs in both. Flowering begins in the dry season and continues well into the rainy season, when the scarlet sprays are frequently the only stab of bright colour on the green canvas.

Semi-evergreen forest is now restricted mainly to the south coast near Moruga, but evergreen forest is much more widespread, and various types may be seen in the Trinity hills, the Arena reserve, the Central Range reserve and the Melajo reserve. The most notable community is the mora forest which occupies large areas north-east of Sangre Grande and also near Guayaguayare. The mora is a tall tree, over 120 feet, and is characterized by enormous plank-like buttresses which may extend six feet from the bole. It is also gregarious and supplies eighty-five to ninety-five per cent of the trees forming the canopy layer. In other parts of the evergreen forest crappo, another useful timber tree, is one of the dominant species.

In these forests a ground layer is virtually absent and the soil is bare or covered with fallen leaves. But shrubs of the coffee and clove families and various species of *Miconia*, collectively called 'sardine', compete for space between the trunks of the large trees, and small palms such as the anari extend their graceful fronds into the languid shade. Along the streams and ravines ferns, selaginellas and spathiphyllum grow in great luxuriance. Everywhere the balisier thrusts on the attention its ostentatious Wagnerian inflorescences.

These and the montane forests of the higher slopes are the home of the game animals, deer, lappe, agouti, quenk, armadillo, which feed on the fallen fruit of the forest trees and distribute their seed. Most of these animals are nocturnal or secretive and unlikely to be seen by the casual visitor. In fact, nearly all the Trinidad mammals are nocturnal: the wood dog, the manicou, the tiger cat, the ant-eater, the numerous species of rat and, of course, the bats. The little sac-winged bat may be seen coursing up and down the forest paths by day, but all the others save their activity for twilight and nighttime hours.

All the small rodents, and even the larger game like quenk and deer, are preyed on by snakes. Pre-eminent among these are the boas but these useful creatures do not restrict their attentions to the native species. They devour as well the introduced rats that abound in plantations, thus rendering good service to agriculture. There are four of them, the rainbow boa, Cook's tree boa (cascabel), the common boa constrictor or macajuel, and the anaconda. The last named, some twenty-five feet in maximum length, is more at home in water than on land and is more or less confined to swampy areas. The two pit vipers, the mapipire zanana (bushmaster) and the mapipire balsin (fer-de-lance) are equally at home in the mountain forests as in the lowland seasonal forests. The only fer-de-lance I have ever seen in the wild was coiled at the side of the path close to the summit of El Tucuche. Though I have never seen a bushmaster in the wild, the species is widespread in all forested regions, particularly the northern range, where they live in the burrows of lappe and armadillo. These two snakes are extremely venomous and therefore highly dangerous, though men have been know to recover from their bites. There are two other poisonous snakes, the corals, one small and common even near Port of Spain, and the other larger and less common. They are both beautifully marked in black, red and white rings that encircle the body. They are less dangerous than the pit vipers because of their small fangs and lesser inclination to bite. Both feed on other snakes.

Among these others are many that are mistaken for the dangerous snakes. The harmless and very common annulated night snake is usually killed on sight as a young mapipire, and so are the clouded snake and the mapipire corde violon. All are brown with a pattern of darker splotches and superficially resemble a mapipire; so much so, that for one of them the word 'mapipire' is used. However, none is venomous. The annulated night snake and the mapipire corde violon live mainly on lizards and frogs, the clouded snake on slugs. There are other snakes that are mistaken for corals and likewise killed, but most people are so terrified of snakes that they will kill on sight any snake regardless of species. But apart from the venomous species, most of the non-poisonous species will not even bite when handled. Among them are real beauties like the green and yellow lora and the black and orange beh-belle chemin.

Trinidad is rich in birds — over four hundred species — with many South American families represented which are not found in the other Caribbean islands. Some of them like the trogons, motmots and antbirds are typically forest birds. Tanagers and flycatchers, common on other Caribbean islands, are common here too. Some have adapted themselves well to man and are as common in town, village and plantation as in their original home.*

Lizards are not conspicuous in the forests. The common ground lizard, the zandolie, is widespread in all types of country from suburban garden to forest and from sea level to at least 1,000 feet in the hills, and will probably be seen on any excursion into the bush. Several lizards of the gekko families are there, but they secrete themselves in the peeling bark of the tree trunks or the crevices of a limestone outcrop. The largest gekko, the wood slave, a harmless and gentle animal, is feared by many, seemingly because of the tenacity with which it can adhere to even the smoothest of surfaces. Folklore predicts dire consequences for anyone unfortunate enough to have a wood slave cling to him.

* Mr ffrench deals with them in a separate chapter. Eds.

The 'twenty-four hour', a medium-sized iguanid lizard, also has an evil reputation in folklore: if one jumps on a person it may cause death within twenty-four hours. In fact, the lizard is completely harmless and is very sluggish in its movements, never jumping and preferring to rely for protection on its concealing colouration rather than on any show of aggression. It becomes quite tame in captivity and can be reared as a pet. The iguana, a miniature dinosaur in appearance but a large lizard in reality, is the only vegetarian lizard and its flesh is esteemed a delicacy.

Frogs and toads abound during the wet season. The large marine toad is surely familiar to everyone. It breeds throughout the year but its great booming call is heard mainly at the two peaks of spawning, one early in the rainy season and one in March, often the driest month of the year. Some frogs have strange ways. *Leptodactylus sibilatrix* lays its eggs in froth nests under stones some distance from water, into which rain eventually washes the tadpoles. *Phyllomedusa trinitatis* selects a bush overhanging a forest pool and lays its eggs into a conical nest that it fashions from a leaf or two as the eggs are being laid. The sticky mucilage surrounding the eggs holds the leaves together until the eggs hatch, when the mucilage dissolves and the tadpoles drop into the water. *Phyllobates trinitatis* lives in the streams of the northern range and its insistent 'chi-chink' may be heard by anyone who travels the north coast road to Maracas Bay. It, too, lays its eggs away from water in crevices in damp rock, and the male transports the tadpoles on his back to their eventual home in the stream.

Of insects I can mention only a few. Butterflies of many kinds abound,* some of spectacular brilliance such as the emperor whose iridescent blue shines gem-like in the shade of a forest path. Termites tunnel busily underground and construct roofed runways to their large globular nests in the trees. Bachac ants plod by the thousand along their well-kept highways, strip the vegetation of its foliage with

* In fact, over 600 species of butterflies occur in Trinidad, and over 120 in Tobago. Eds.

neat semicircular incisions and transport the severed bits to their nest, there to chew them into a mulch. On this mulch the ants cultivate the fungus that is their sole food. Army ants swarm out in eager columns in their search for prey, their forays controlled by their nomadic habits and the exigencies of their breeding cycle. Wasps attach to the face of a cliff or the aerial root of an epiphyte their delicate vase-like cells or clustered tubules of mud, or suspend their fragile paper nests from the lower surface of leaf or limb. Any large leaf overhanging a path may conceal a wasps' nest and a careless contact with it can produce highly unpleasant results. Mosquitoes can be a nuisance, and worse than wasps or mosquitoes is the bête rouge, the larval form of a mite, so minute it is barely visible. It burrows into the skin to feed and the irritation this causes raises bumps of exquisite itchiness that become all too evident only the day after the excursion.

Trinidad's rivers are seldom fished for sport though more frequently fished for food. Among the twenty or more food fishes, only three are at all important, the cascadura, the guabine and the yarrow. (The cascadura, an armoured catfish, is reputedly of so fine a flavour that the visitor who once tastes its flesh must return to Trinidad to end his days.) Fishing for the aquarium trade is, on the other hand, a thriving industry. The species most in demand are the teta and the pui-pui, but some of the more colourful characins, such as the featherfin and the sword-tail tetra, are also exported. Trinidad is, too, the home of the guppy. Known to the average Trinidadian as 'millions' and now known scientifically as *Lebistes reticulatus*, the first specimens from Trinidad were named *Girardinus guppyi* in honour of Mr Lechmere Guppy, our most notable ichthyologist of a hundred years ago and, as guppies, they are now bred in countless aquaria throughout the world. Since they will thrive in heavily polluted streams and drains and feed voraciously on mosquito larvae, guppies in their native land are important allies of man in his incessant war against mosquito-borne diseases. The jumping guabine, because of its ability to travel overland, is widely distributed and the only fish to inhabit the clear streams of the more mountainous regions.

Above the 1,000 feet level the hills of the northern range are clothed in montane forests. Lower montane rain forests occur on the lower levels, and true cloud forest above 2,500 feet, on the Aripo massif. Some trees more typical of seasonal forest, such as poui, cypre and hogplum, stray into the lower zone. There are relatively few lianes here and epiphytes are confined to the canopy. Ground vegetation is sparse. In the true cloud forest, however, lianes festoon the trees in great luxuriance, and epiphytes of many types — bromeliads, orchids, aroids, ferns — vie with one another for space. Palms and ferns form an under-storey and tree ferns are well represented. At the very top of Mount Aripo is the elfin woodland — silent, mist-shrouded, remote. This strange vegetation is dominated by small palms and tree ferns. Every available surface is covered with moss and lichen and water drips perpetually into the saturated earth.

In these high mountain forests special forms of life appear. Thus, the golden tree frog lives out its life cycle in the leaf bases of only a few species of bromeliad and only at the summit of El Tucuche (3,072 feet). So far as I know, its voice, if it has one, has never been heard by man. Its strange bedfellows in the bromeliad* are a cockroach and a scorpion. Presumably, both frog and scorpion prey on the cockroach. Another tiny frog of the montane forests is *Nototheca Fitzgeraldi* for which there is no common name. It overcomes the problem of breeding by incubating up to six eggs in a brood pouch in the back of the female. The tadpoles leave the egg pouch in an advanced stage of development and live for just a few days in water that has collected in the leaf bases of bromeliads or aroids before metamorphosing to the adult form.

Limestone areas support forests that differ slightly from those of other areas, but more noteworthy are the caves that occur in limestone, and the animals that inhabit them. The most famous of these caves are at Aripo and Oropouche. Both are occupied by thousands of bats of several species and by the extraordinary guacharo, a large cave-bird with

* A favourite place of abode is the giant bromeliad, *Glomeropitcairnia erectiflora*, the largest wildpine in the New World. Eds.

a wing span of three to three and a half feet. It was in a small cave in the Aripo area that Ivan Sanderson came upon a new species of lizard hiding in a cleft in the rock. He describes the capture as follows: 'Instead of running out it turned its head away from me and both its sides lit up for a few seconds like the portholes on a ship. Eventually, I got it out with forceps, and as I held it up, it again lit up brilliantly.' This lizard was subsequently named *Proctoporus shrevei*. Since then others have collected it on El Tucuche but no one has ever observed luminescence. Was Sanderson mistaken? Only time will tell.

The highest mountain tops in Trinidad are just over 3,000 feet; the lowest depths are below sea level and support swamp communities of various kinds. On the east coast is the large Nariva swamp, some 30,000 acres in extent. It is a fresh-water swamp in the Manzanilla area emptying to the sea by the Nariva River which runs parallel to the shore for some two or three miles. The margins support palm forests dominated by the royal palm on the seaward side and the moriche palm on the landward side. The inner reaches of the swamp are choked with the giant herbs, *Montrichardia* and *Cyperus*. The tender unexpanded leaves of *Montrichardia* supply the food for the caterpillars of a very pretty little butterfly with hind wings like shields of highly polished embossed metal.

This complex of swamp communities exists elsewhere in Trinidad, but Nariva is the largest and possibly the most fascinating. Parrots congregate in large noisy flocks and the colourful but rare macaws occur nowhere else. Troupes of red howler monkeys, vocal but secretive and melancholy, swing though the trees that surround the swamp proper. In the water lurk anacondas large enough to swallow whole a six-foot alligator. Manatee have been seen there. Fish abound and two unusual amphibians occur in large numbers. The Surinam toad, although entirely aquatic, finds it necessary to raise its young in pockets in the female's back. The paradox frog does most of its growing in the tadpole stage so that the enormous tadpole, some nine inches long when full grown, shrinks at metamorphosis to an almost adult-sized frog of only two and a half inches.

Where the sea has access to the low-lying land, the swamp is a brackish-water swamp rather than a fresh-water one and supports a very different community composed almost entirely of mangroves. Such is the Caroni swamp, home of the scarlet ibis. This spectacular inhabitant, large and brilliantly scarlet with contrasting black primaries, can be seen at almost any time of the year but is most numerous in the breeding season from April to August. Skeins of graceful, gliding birds, their bodies burnished by the rays of a dying sun, make a rapturous sight as they streak homeward from their feeding grounds against a sky of cobalt blue. Their food consists mainly of crabs which they seek out on the mud flats exposed at low tide, and on the stilt roots of the red mangrove. Innumerable other birds such as egrets, herons, ducks, plovers, sandpipers and rails, live and feed in the swamp. Some are migrants remaining with us but a short time, before nature urges them on their way again, whereas others are indigenous and reside here the year round.

In certain parts of Trinidad the flat lands are poorly drained and are seasonally waterlogged. One such area in the triangle Valencia — Guaico — Cumuto exemplifies all the vegetation forms that may arise. Near the Valencia-Guaico Road, there is the highly specialized marsh forest in which about half of all the individual plants are palms, mostly of three species, palma real, timite and manac, with occasional specimens of two others, cocorite and moriche. The last named is typical of the palm marsh that fringes the worst drained patches on which only a tree-less savannah is possible. Fine examples can be seen on the edges of the Aripo Savannah. The open savannahs themselves, though poor in vegetation, are fascinating. They are remnants of the llanos which stretch through the middle regions of Venezuela. The soil is almost devoid of nutrients so the plants have evolved special adaptions. The most bizarre are the insect traps of the bladderworts and sundew. The bladderwort consists of little more than a tuft of roots and a fragile flower stalk bearing a pretty purplish flower. Interspersed on the roots are the hollow swellings or bladders that trap and digest tiny soil-dwelling insects. The sundew is a rosette of leaves, hardly more that

This hummingbird obligingly nested in Norman Parkinson's garden in Tobago.

three inches across, growing on the exposed soil. Each leaf is covered with club-shaped glands that secrete a viscous fluid sticky enough to trap any small insect that may alight on it. Once trapped the insect is dissolved by digestive juices. Parasitism is another adaptation to the severe conditions, and the love vine stretches its all-embracing orange tentacles throughout the grassy area. Strangely enough, birds are common, especially in the tree islands, and one may see manakins, woodpeckers, finches, the soldier bird and even hummingbirds.

One of the common trees of the palm marsh which rejoices in the imaginative local name of fatpork, is also a common and characteristic species of the sea shore in association with the sea-side grape whose graceful, fan-shaped leaves form the perfect background to the inviting beach. Behind the sandy shore and in the muddy banks of the river mouths, the blue crabs tunnel out their homes, ever watchful, never straying too far from their means of escape. Male fiddler crabs stand before their burrows and solicit the attention of the females with the waving motion of the large claw that has earned them their everyday name. Out on the shining sands the ghost crabs scurry back and forth, wraith-like, as they are disturbed at their incessant digging. In the ocean beyond the shore line live the myriad creatures of the sea, turtles, fishes, molluscs, sea crabs, jelly-fish, even porpoises sometimes, all interesting and colourful in their own way but hardly specifically Trinidadian. In earlier times, one of these was especially important, the humble chip-chip, an inconspicuous bivalve mollusc that spends most of its life buried in the sand between high and low-water marks. Their delicately coloured shells, now bleached and faded, may be found by the thousand in mounds well back from the shore, discarded in the kitchen middens of the aboriginal Indian inhabitants for whom the chip-chip was the staple item of food. These were the people who watched from the shore as Columbus's tiny fleet sailed along the southern coast; these were the people who bequeathed to us, their successors, the rich natural flora and fauna, scarcely disturbed by their activities in search of food and living space. Half a millennium has passed; the changes have been many; roads,

Top: Cacrico, the second of Trinidad and Tobago's national birds. Bottom: Motmot or king of the forest. Both photographed at Mrs Alefounder's house in Tobago, where bird-lovers are made welcome.

factories, dwelling houses have reduced the original vegetation and changed it: but Trinidad is still a land as beautiful and green as the gardens of Valencia. May it long remain so!

Alphabetical List of Plant Names

Anari palm	*Geonoma vaga*
Balisier	*Heleconia bihai*
Black poui	*Tabebuia rufescens*
Black-stick	*Pachystachys coccinea*
Bladderwort	*Utriculuria spp.*
Bois lezard	*Tecoma stans*
Cannonball	*Couroupita guianensis*
Cedar	*Cedrela mexicana*
Chaconia	*Warsewiczia coccinea*
Cocorite palm	*Maximiliana elegans*
Crappo	*Carapa guianensis*
Cypre	*Cordia alliodora*
Fatpork	*Crysobalanus icaco*
Hogplum	*Spondias mombin*
Immortelle	*Erythrina micropteryx*
Manac	*Euterpe langloisii*
Mora	*Mora excelsa*
Moriche palm	*Mauritia setigera*
Palma real	*Jessenia oligocarpa*
Purpleheart	*Peltogyne porphyrocardia*
Red mangrove	*Rhizophera mangle*
Royal palm	*Roystonea oleracea*
Seaside grape	*Cocoloba uvifera*
Silk cotton	*Ceiba pentandra*
Spathiphyllum	*Spathiphyllum cannifolium*
Sundew	*Drosera capillaris*
Sweet lime	*Murraya exotica*
Tantakayo	*Albizzia caribaea*
Timite	*Manicaria saccifera*
Yellow poui	*Tabebuia serratifolia*

Alphabetical List of Animal Names

Agouti	*Dasyprocta aguti*
Alligator	*Caiman sclerops*
Anaconda	*Eunectes murinus*
Annulated night snake	*Leptodeira annulata*
Ant-eater	*Tamandura longicauda*
Armadillo	*Tatusia novemcincta*
Army ants	*Eciton spp.*
Bachac ants	*Atta cephalotes* *Acromyrmex octospinosus*
Lappe	*Coelogenys paca*
Large coral snake	*Micrurus lemniscatus*
Macajuel	*Boa constrictor*
Manatee	*Manatus manatus*
Manicou	*Didelphis marsupialis*
Mapipire balsin	*Bothrops atrox*
Mapipire corde violon	*Imantodes chencoa*

Beh-belle chemin	*Leimadophis melanotus*
Blue crab	*Cardiosoma guanhumi*
Bushmaster	*Lachesis muta*
Cascabel	*Boa enydris cooki*
Cascadura	*Hoplosternum littorale*
Chip-chip	*Donax striatus; Donax denticulatus*
Clouded snake	*Sibon nebulatus*
Cook's tree boa	*Boa enydris cooki*
Deer	*Mazama rufa*
Emperor	*Morpho peleides insularis*
Featherfin	*Hemigrammus unilineatus*
Fer-de-lance	*Bothrops atrox*
Fiddler crabs	*Uca spp.*
Ghost crab	*Oxypode quadrata*
Golden tree frog	*Amphodus auratus*
Guabine	*Hoplias malabaricus*
Guacharo	*Steatornis caripensis*
Iguana	*Iguana iguana*
Jumping guabine	*Rivulus hartii*
Mapipire zanana	*Lachesis muta*
Marine toad	*Bufo marinus*
Paradox frog	*Pseudis paradoxa*
Pui-pui	*Corydoras aeneus*
Quenk	*Dicotyles tajacu*
Rainbow boa	*Epicrates cenchris*
Red howler	*Alouatta insulanus*
Sac-winged bat	*Saccopteryx bilineata*
Scarlet ibis	*Eudocimus ruber*
Small coral snake	*Micrurus circinalis*
Surinam toad	*Pipa pipa*
Sword-tail tetra	*Corynopoma riisei*
Teta	*Hypostomus plecostomus*
Tiger cat	*Leopardus pardalis*
Twentyfour hours	*Polychrus marmoratus*
Wood dog	*Tayra barbara*
Wood slave	*Thecadactylus rapicauda*
Yarrow	*Hoplerythrinus unitaeniatus*

The Birds

Richard P. ffrench

Visitors to a tropical island undoubtedly expect to see beautiful birds with gaudy plumage flying about the place. Such birds certainly exist in Trinidad and Tobago, but you have to know where to look and how to find them. A certain amount will depend, of course, on what sort of visitor you are, and how much trouble you are prepared to take in your quest.

Almost every visitor has at least a faint interest in the natural history of the land he is visiting. Even those with none will want to see the famous, the beautiful, and the exciting sights of the place. Here in Trinidad the birds make their special contribution in the Caroni swamp, where the magnificent scarlet ibis (*Eudocimus ruber*) — locally known as 'flamingo' — makes its home. Several thousands of these brilliant scarlet birds nest and roost in an area of the swamp — set aside by the Government as a sanctuary — and may be seen there at any time of the year. Boats with experienced guides leave daily in mid-afternoon from Port of Spain and the northern section of the Princess Margaret Highway. Unless it is the nesting season the birds will not be seen in large numbers until they flock in to roost in a traditional spot during the last two hours of daylight. The breath-taking beauty of the spectacle, with thousands of scarlet birds wheeling in the blue sky against a background of green mangroves, is almost beyond description.

A very different experience awaits the visitor to Tobago, if he makes the expedition to Tobago's off-shore islet of Little Tobago at the north-eastern end of the island. Here in a specially appointed sanctuary live greater birds of paradise (*Paradisea apoda*), the descendants of birds imported from New Guinea in the early years of this century. Here, in the only part of the New World where birds of paradise roam wild, these great birds can be seen without much difficulty. Boats leave daily from Speyside, but once on the island the visitor should expect to walk, for the birds are shy. However, a knowledgeable guide is available, and a sight of the excitingly-coloured male bird performing his courtship ceremony is worth the little effort required.

Trinidad is sometimes referred to as the 'Land of the Hummingbird'. The source of the claim perhaps lies in the fact that no fewer than sixteen different species of humming-birds have been found within this one small island. Most live in the forest, but many can be seen feeding at garden flowers or at the blossoms of flowering trees like the mountain immortelle, the yellow poui or the flamboyant. It must be remembered, however, that humming-birds are so tiny — some hardly three inches long — that they are difficult to observe without binoculars, especially since their movements are so rapid. In addition, their brilliant iridescent plumage does not show up to advantage unless you are positioned at the right angle, preferably on a higher level.

Visitors generally ask a little more than just to see the bird life. They want to know the names of these creatures. There is much to learn about the birds of Trinidad and Tobago, and even a single drive through the countryside will put you in touch with many interesting and beautiful species. Even in the city of Port of Spain you can't miss the kiskadee (*Pitangus sulphuratus*), the brown and yellow flycatcher with black and white striped head, whose lusty, raucous cry — variously interpreted in different countries, but translated here as '*Qu'est ce qu'il dit?*' — rings out from dawn to dusk. In gardens and parks you will see the longtailed tropical mockingbird (*Mimus gilvus*), sometimes called day clean, who makes up for his nondescript grey colouring by the beauty of his singing. Also common in these areas is the ruddy ground-dove (*Columbina talpacoti*), locally known as zortolan, a tiny pigeon that feeds on the ground, usually in pairs. If you are staying near the sea in Tobago you will undoubtedly notice the enormous brown pelican (*Pelecanus occidentalis*), known to West Indians as grand gosier, as he dives for fish just offshore. Often a crowd of laughing gulls (*Larus atricilla*) accompanies him, to perch on his head and cheekily grab their share of his catch. Across the road flashes a vision of blue wings as the blue-grey tanager (*Thraupis episcopus*) or blue jean seeks its favourite fruit tree. In the garden, less colourful but conspicuous by its behaviour, the blue-black grassquit (*Volatinia jacarina*) or *ci-ci zeb* whiles away the hours with his strange courtship performance. Known also as Johnny-jump-up, this tiny, glossy black finch leaps up from his perch a foot or two and somersaults back into position, uttering at the same time his wheezing cry. The display is evidently for the benefit of his dull brown mate, even though she may not be apparent nearby.

If you drive through the countryside, you should have no difficulty in finding a nesting colony of the crested oropendola (*Psarocolius decumanus*) or yellowtail cornbird. The nests, long stocking-shaped baskets slung from the branches of a tall tree, swing in the breeze. The bird enters through a hole in the top and wriggles down perhaps six feet to the nest-chamber in the bottom. In display these oropendolas hang upside down from their perch, uttering a variety of strange clucks and gobblings. If your journey carries you through the east or south of Trinidad, you should find numbers of the large orangewinged parrot (*Amazona amazonica*) flying about the edges of the forest or over the cultivated areas. Almost invariably found in pairs or family parties, these parrots fill the air with their strange, raucous screams. Though to the casual listener these cries sound the same all over Trinidad, in fact several 'dialects' have been discovered in the various parts of the island.

Many country people like to keep cage-birds and will proudly display their pets to a visitor. Commonest are the beautiful semp (*Euphonia violaceus*) which is a small fruit-eating tanager, and the grey seedeater (*Sporophila intermedia*) or picoplat, a dull bird with an exuberant, chattering song. Other species of finches and parrots may also be found in captivity. Since many of Trinidad's most beautiful species are insect-eaters, they are rarely seen in captivity except in zoos with special facilities.

Visitors to the Caroni swamp should not allow themselves to be blinded by the spectacular scarlet ibis to the beauty and variety of the many other swamp and marsh birds. Well over 100 species have been recorded within the Caroni swamp alone. Most prominent are the herons and egrets which share the roost with the ibis. The most interesting of the white egrets, and probably the most numerous, is the cattle egret (*Ardeola ibis*), which was unknown in Trinidad before 1950. It is believed that this species, common in tropical areas of Africa and Asia, crossed the Atlantic Ocean earlier in this century and formed colonies in parts of northern South America. Gradually the population expanded through the Caribbean and south-eastern USA, since the bird found an ecological niche unfilled by other species. It habitually feeds on grasshoppers and other large insects, and frequently accompanies cattle and other grazing animals, seizing the insects as they are disturbed by the animals, truly a boon to farmers. Another spectacular and conspicuous bird to be found in freshwater sections of the area is the wattled jacana (*Jacana spinosa*) or spur-wing; this long-legged marsh-dweller has reddish brown plumage with primrose-yellow wings which it displays only in flight as it flutters or glides low over the lilies and reeds where it lives. It has enormous long toes, which enable it to walk with ease upon the floating vegetation of marsh pools and creeks. On the bend of its wing (and not seen except at close quarters) is a wicked-looking spur, capable of inflicting a painful wound upon an attacker, so that hunters keep their dogs away from this bird whenever possible.

Tobago has its own particular charms among the bird life, especially because birds always seem to be more confiding and easy to approach here than in other areas.* No visitor can miss the tiny yellow-breasted bananaquit (*Coereba flaveola*) or sucrier, as it cheekily perches on his hotel dining-table to raid the sugar bowl. Then there is the glossy black carib grackle (*Quiscalus lugubris*) with his long keel-

* A close acquaintance with many of the birds of Tobago, notably the cocrico and the motmot, may be made at the house of Mrs Alefounder, Grafton Estate. She has established her verandah as a feeding-place, to which birds flock in perfect confidence, and she graciously allows visitors who share her interest in birds to come any afternoon and watch. No appointment need be made. You need only drive up and ask, and offer the birds and your hostess the respect of quietness.

shaped tail, who struts importantly about the yard or verandah picking up scraps. A drive through the Tobago countryside is sure to bring you face to face with the blue-crowned motmot (*Momotus momota*) or king of the woods. This beautifully coloured species has an extraordinary tail. The long central feathers are racquet-tipped — that is, the feather vanes near the end of the tail are weak and fall away from the shaft, leaving the shaft bare for an inch or so, tipped by a normally feathered section. As the bird flies, it seems to be followed by a black blob. Closely related to the motmot is the rufous-tailed jacamar (*Galbula ruficauda*) or king hummingbird, which is also quite commonly found at the roadsides in Tobago. Looking indeed like a very large hummingbird with its brilliant iridescent plumage of golden-green and reddish-brown, the jacamar swoops gracefully out from its perch to catch butterflies, dragonflies and other large flying insects which most other birds cannot catch. Returning to its perch, it batters the victim to death, removing the indigestible wings. Both motmots and jacamars nest in holes in roadside banks — the motmot being known to tunnel as far as fourteen feet into a bank.

Tobago's national bird is the rufous-tailed chachalaca (*Ortalis ruficauda*) — better known as the cocrico. More often heard than seen, this turkey-like bird sounds its loud, grating chorus, especially at dawn and dusk, mainly in the higher areas of the island amidst forest or the dry scrubby lands bordering cultivated areas. In some areas, however, cocricos approach quite close to human habitation.

One of Tobago's special bird attractions is the variety of sea-birds to be found around the shores. One of the most spectacular is the red-billed tropic-bird (*Phaethon aethereus*) — known to most Tobagonians as booby, as arc all sea-birds. On a visit to Little Tobago you must ask the guide to show you the tropic-birds. At most seasons of the year they will be found soaring and gliding off the steep, craggy cliffs where they nest, large white birds with strong red beaks and long, delicate tails, masters of the air in the strongest breeze. Extraordinarily tenacious sitters at the nest, they will allow anyone fortunate enough to come across an accessible nest to take photographs from the c'osest distance without leaving their egg or chick.

For the visitor who may wish to explore deeper into the wealth of our islands' bird-life there is plenty of scope. Over 400 species have been recorded in Trinidad and Tobago, the great majority in Trinidad, while the smaller island alone boasts a list of over 150 species. The proximity of Trinidad to the mainland of South America — a mere eight miles separating it at the closest point from Venezuela — and the diversity of its environment, with mountain rain-forest, mangrove swamp, seashore and savannah country all present in a small area, combine to produce ecological conditions suitable for a large variety of species. In addition, Trinidad's position places it at a cross-roads of bird migration; for winter visitors from the north pass through or stay for a few months, whilst several other species migrate from the south of South America to this area, escaping from the southern winter between May and September.

To see more than a few of the islands' birds, however, the visitor must be prepared to go to some trouble, effort and expense. Contacts can be made through the Trinidad Field Naturalists' Club or the Asa Wright Nature Centre near Arima, and most important of all an experienced guide can be found to assist the visitor with advice or personal direction. Some taxi-drivers have quite a considerable knowledge of the islands' natural history, but most will know only the really common species of general interest. In conclusion, then, here are a few ideas to help the visitor know some of the more unusual, but no less interesting, facets of Trinidad and Tobago's bird life.

Living by day in pitch-dark caves and feeding at night on the fruits of palms and other oil-bearing trees, the oil-bird (*Steatornis caripensis*) or guacharo is one of Trinidad's most fascinating birds. There are only a few caves in the island where these birds live, some on private lands such as at Springhill in the Arima valley, or the Oropouche cave in the Platanal. Permission must be obtained from the landowners to visit these caves. Others are on the sea-coast or high on the slopes of Mount Cerro del Aripo, Trinidad's highest mountain. An experienced guide may be found in Aripo village to take parties to these caves.

Many trails exist among the mountains of the Northern Range, and the enthusiastic bird-watcher will want to try some of them out. Trails leading from the Caura valley or from Ortinola in the Maracas valley carry one high up on to Mount El Tucuche, where a wealth of bird-life exists. Here one should find the display-grounds of the white-bearded manakin (*Manacus manacus*) or casse-noisette, where the tiny black and white male birds perform various antics on low saplings, each beside his private 'court' — a cleared patch of forest floor a few inches square — while they whine and snap at each other like animated fire-crackers. At other display grounds will be found groups of male humming-birds — known as hermits — sitting low in the undergrowth, singing their short snatches of song in rivalry for most of the day and posturing in strange attitudes. With a little luck the hiker will catch a glimpse of the channel-billed toucan (*Ramphastos vitellinus*) with its enormous bill, as it hops about the tree-tops in search of fruit. Many forest sounds will be heard, including the loud 'tock' of the bearded bellbird (*Procnias averano*) or campanero, whose other call sounds like the tolling of an old cracked bell. In the remoter parts of the Northern Range, east of Aripo and Blanchisseuse, where trails are few and a guide essential, one might be lucky enough to come across the rare white bellbird (*Procnias alba*), or the Trinidad piping-guan (*Pipile pipile*) paoui or pawi — the only endemic species found in Trinidad, now so rare that few have seen it. Another rarity, known in this remote area, is the scaled ant-pitta (*Grallaria guatemalensis*), known to science by only a handful of specimens from Trinidad.

Such trips are for the most adventurous. Easier excursions will be down the east coast to the Nariva swamp, where at the south-eastern edge in the evening flocks of red-bellied macaws (*Ara manilata*) fly in to feed in the cabbage palms. With luck one might see a few individuals of the great blue-and-yellow macaw (*Ara ararauna*), now unfortunately very rare in Trinidad. Down in the savannah area of the Oropouche lagoon, near San Fernando, bird enthusiasts will be astonished by the vast flocks of visiting dickcissels (*Spiza americana*) which between January and mid-April each year feed in the area. Gathering into huge flocks at about 5 p.m. each evening these small finches fly to their roosts in neighbouring canefields, where they collect in tens of thousands. Another spectacular bird at the roost is the fork-tailed flycatcher (*Muscivora tyrannus*) or scissors-tail, also a visitor, this time from Argentina, which between May and October gathers in countless numbers into its roost in the Caroni swamp.

For those who are enthusiastic about sea-birds these two adventures are well worth while. One from Trinidad is to Soldado Rock, a few miles off the south-western tip of the island. Here, between March and July, can be found thousands of nesting sea-birds, in particular the sooty tern (*Sterna fuscata*) and the brown noddy (*Anous stolidus*). The birds lie so thickly on the ground that one has to be careful to avoid stepping on eggs and young. A boat can be chartered from Icacos or Cedros, but it is advisable for the visitor to settle the charges in advance, which after a little friendly bargaining should not be unreasonable. From Tobago an even more exciting trip can be made to the St Giles islands, off the north-eastern tip of Tobago, where various species of sea-birds nest, including the magnificent frigatebird (*Fregata magnificens*) or man-o'-war, the red-footed booby (*Sula sula*), and the brown booby (*Sula leucogaster*), Audubon's shearwater (*Puffinus lherminieri*), and various species of terns and tropicbirds. To get to St Giles one leaves by boat from Speyside or Charlotteville, but it is a longish journey, possibly in choppy waters. Also one cannot land without a special permit from the Forestry Division; both St Giles and Soldado Rock are wild-life sanctuaries. However, even a trip around St Giles is spectacular, and the fishing is very good too.

One of the commonest birds of both islands is the smooth-billed ani (*Crotophaga ani*) or merle corbeau, which makes communal nests and brings up the young under a kind of kibbutz system. The ani itself is a grotesque black bird with a ridged beak and a long tail, and provokes both amusement at its ungainly antics and interest in its complicated social organization. In the night various owls and night jars call, and if you stay near the forest or swamp you may hear the melancholy notes of the potoo (*Nyctibius griseus*) or poor-me-one. During the day this strange night-bird sits upright and motionless on a stump, perfectly camouflaged as it merges with the dead wood. But at night if you approach it with a strong flashlight its great red eyes gleam in reflection like twin lanterns before it flits off after its meal of moths.

One can see then, that there is ample opportunity in our islands for the energetic and enterprising visitor interested in bird life, and there is enough in this interesting field to keep such a visitor enthralled, however long his stay may be.

The Food

Therese Mills

When the English writer, Charles Kingsley, visited Port of Spain in 1870 he described the Queen's Park Savannah as 'a public park and race ground such as neither London nor Paris can boast'.

His enthusiasm was understandable. Against a background of lush mountain range he saw an expanse of green acres on which cattle grazed. He saw lovers strolling arm in arm across the crisp green turf or sitting in the shade of the giant saman trees. He saw nursemaids pushing carriages with rosy cheeked babies peeping out from between the white frills.

It wasn't long after Kingsley's visit that the Savannah, spread over 199 acres, began to lose some of its tranquillity. Football and cricket clubs moved in, staking out claims to this or that piece of ground. Tramcars appeared too, clattering round and round on their iron rails like a merry-go-round at a country fair. There appeared, too, 'Mile-a-Minute', a Chinese peanut vendor who, like the tramcar, lapped the three-mile circumference of the Savannah with dizzying frequency. Slung over his arm he carried a basket with small packets of peanuts which he sold at two cents each.

By now the halcyon days are nearly over. The cattle have disappeared (though race-horses are ridden out to exercise in the cool of the very early morning). So, too, have the tramcars, now replaced by a never-ending stream of motor cars. Their occupants, unlike Kingsley, seem less interested in the natural beauty of this park than in the wide variety of food that it is now possible to buy 'around the Savannah'.

'Mile-a-Minute' has long since joined his Venerable Ancestors but his pioneering zeal lives on in the many vendors who have set up businesses on the periphery of the park. Indeed, could Kingsley see it today, sentimentalist though he was, he would probably feel compelled to comment on its culinary charms.

Trinidadians are noted for their care-free, fun-loving approach to life, but when it comes to food they are very serious. They live to eat and they love going out in the evening for 'something' to eat. Which is why on any evening round the Savannah today one can enjoy what must be regarded as a four course meal, eaten either in the privacy of one's car parked along the Pitch Walk, or sitting astride the iron railings that surround the park.

Begin with an Oyster Cocktail.

These oysters grow on trees — more precisely they grow on the roots of the mangrove in the swamps outside Port of Spain. At ebb tide the retreating sea exposes the oysters and it is a simple matter to pick them off. The oyster vendor stands behind a tray on which the oysters, still in their shells, are piled high in pyramid fashion. Standing like sentinels alongside the shells are bottles of 'dressing'. These include hot pepper sauce, tomato ketchup, and vinegar.

Mark you, the vendor would look surprised if you asked for an oyster cocktail. The thing to do is to walk casually up to him, hands preferably in pockets, and say:

'Start opening!'

He starts opening.

Using a short-blade knife and with an expert twist of the hand, he deals with the oyster shells faster than you can think. You may prefer them in a glass with the dressing well mixed in, or you may prefer to 'slurp' each one individually with your tongue from the shell as you go along. The oysters are small and succulent, their flavour pronounced but delicate, and it is possible to eat dozens of them without even noticing. But don't worry, oysters are famous in Trinidad for their aphrodisiac quality; they can do you only good.

Next comes the fish course. This is usually a thick slice of fried shark which is sandwiched, hamburger-style, in a roll of 'hops' bread. The vendor has an unusual sign that informs the customer:

'In God We Trust
Everyone Else Cash'

so have your money ready. And cast aside any prejudice concerning shark. It is quite delicious and goes down well with the 'hops', which is round like a large bun but more like French bread in that there is more crust to it than crumb. The shark is sprinkled with a good helping of hot pepper sauce and you bite into it much as you would into a hamburger, except that the uninitiated and small-of-mouth may find it a bit unwieldy to start with. You soon get the haog of it.

As a middle course there is a choice of chicken and chips, or roti. The former is sufficiently known to require no description here so we can confine ourselves to the roti, an East Indian dish probably best described as a sort of meat patty. It is essential that it be eaten hot, so it is prepared while you wait.

An outer casing of dough is rolled out thinly and cooked on a red hot platten until it turns slightly brown. Meat, highly seasoned and cooked with curry is placed in the centre and the cooked dough is wrapped around it ready to eat. Roti comes in all flavours — chicken, beef, liver, goat, shrimp and plain potato, but whichever you choose there is no mistaking the strong flavour of Indian curry.

If roti is not for you there is delicious corn on the cob boiled in a rich stock of herbs, and salted meat, meat roasted on open coal-fires. Every vendor has his or her stall lit with a flambeau, which is a wick burning in a bottle of paraffin.

The evening's intake can be washed down with coconut water, available from a donkey cart. With a deft twist of the wrist the vendor swings his cutlass and the head of the coconut is off, so that you can drink its refreshing water straight from the shell.

In case you are wondering how Trinidadians can stomach such a mixture at one sitting, remember that they are a people descended from many different races. Each group of immigrants, when they came, brought its own customs, culture and traditions. Into the Trinidad pot has gone the food not only of the original inhabitants, the Amerindians, but also of the Spaniards and of the French and English settlers who followed them as colonizers; of the Africans who were brought here as slaves; and of the East Indians, the Chinese, the Portuguese and the Syrians. The result is a fine cuisine, rich in flavour, style and technique, which (even more than the sunshine and the blue skies) makes those who leave these shores long for home and the delights of home cooking.

Crab and calaloo, peas and rice, pastelles, pelau, buljol,* crab-backs, black pudding and souse, bakes, float and akra, roti, sancoche and coconut bread: all these can inspire passionate nostalgia. And where else can one drink mauby, sea moss, sorrel and ginger beer, or enjoy the delights of mammy apple and guava jam and coconut ice-cream?

Today we call these dishes Creole food, indicating that though they have been influenced by many cultures they are now our very own. But it is interesting to look back on history.

When Christopher Columbus discovered the island of Trinidad (he missed Tobago) in 1498, it was inhabited by the Arawaks. Cassava, which appears to be indigenous, was one of their basic foods. They used the cassava in much the same way wheat flour in used today. They made bread and cakes with it. But the Amerindians discovered that in the use of cassava caution had to be exercised as there were two varieties — sweet and bitter. The bitter cassava contained a high percentage of prussic acid which was poisonous, and indeed they used it to kill off their enemies. But enterprising as they were, they also discovered that the prussic acid mixed with certain herbs produced 'cassareep', a marvellous preservative which is today used in the making of the famous West Indian 'Pepper Pot'.

Over the years Creole cooks have invented new ways with the cassava. For example, grated raw and mixed with coconut, spices and sugar, it is baked to produce a delicious and tasty 'pone' (or pudding).

The Amerindians also ate much river fish, including the cascadura about which legend has it that he who eats this fish shall always return to Trinidad. Though its magical quality did not save the Amerindian race from extinction here, we

* Buljol: shredded saltfish, chipped onions, tomatoes, diced avocado pear, pepper and olive oil. The name is derived from the French *brûlé* (burnt) and *geule* (slang for mouth), and the dish is a great favourite nowadays. Eds.

Children of Trinidad and Tobago.

go on eating the cascadura and would allow no visitor to leave without sampling its delicate flavour.

Amerindian middens which have been excavated also reveal that they ate large quantities of shell-fish — oysters, shrimp, conch, crab and chip-chip, the same as we do today.

In their day the forests around abounded with wild game which they hunted and roasted. They ate the fruit of palm trees such as the pewah, which is still a delicacy today. In the forests, too, the Amerindians found a red berry and squeezed out the juice to paint war-like images on their faces. It was the roocoo,* still used today, but for a different purpose, that is to flavour and colour meat dishes.

The coming of the Spaniards introduced the first European ideas into our cooking. For example, where the Amerindians had taken the corn on the cob and simply roasted it over an open fire, the Spaniards made pastelles and arepas. A pastelle is best described as a minced-meat patty made with corn flour. The meat filling is highly seasoned and flavoured with chopped olives, capers, raisins and so on. This is placed in a thin corn flour case which is folded. The patty is then wrapped in banana leaves and boiled. The arepa is like pastelle except that it is fried. A well-known expert on local food has said that the old menus of Spanish banquets indicated frequent use of the pastelle.

The Spaniards also began to import food from Europe, mainly beans and dried meat and fish, starting a pattern of food importation that is still with us.

When the French came they brought their own cooks and it was not long before their influence began to leave its mark in the extensive use of herbs and spices**, which is an outstanding feature of Trinidad cooking. Herbs such as chives, onion, thyme and garlic are used in the preparation of almost every dish and many of these herbs are grown in the village of Maraval, where many of the descendants of the Martiniquan cooks still live today.

* Anatto or Roucou (*Bixa orellana*), a small tree, native of South America and the West Indies. Eds.

** To visitors an interesting feature of the enormous covered food market of Port of Spain is the number of little stalls, or corners of stalls, displaying spices which would be considered exotic at home. The lavish abundance of fruit in the market is a fine sight. Eds.

Trinidad and Tobago can still provide solitude and peace.

In addition to the herbs, Creole cooking has added something of its own — the green pepper. Placed whole in the pot and never allowed to burst open and let loose its hot burning spell, it rides and bubbles atop the sizzling stew, the peas and rice, the callaloo, adding an unequalled flavour and aroma.

From the French we got black pudding and souse. Black pudding is a blood sausage highly seasoned and spiced, an accompaniment for souse, which is pigs' trotters marinated in lime-juice, pepper, onion, celery, and vinegar and dressed with sliced cucumber and water-cress. It is a must for Sunday morning breakfast, accompanied by home-made sweet bread.

In their large plantation houses, attended by slaves, the French used to eat meals which were more like feasts. The centrepiece was usually a suckling pig or a large joint of wild meat (as we call game). But while they feasted, their slaves were given rations of cheaper foods imported from Europe, chiefly salted and dried fish and meat. They supplemented this diet with the root vegetables they grew in their small garden plots*. They developed a stew of their own, using the various vegetables, salted meat and coconut milk which is known today as sancoche.**

The slaves also found a use for the leaves of the root vegetablc called dasheen. They boiled them down to a purée — the beginnings of today's calaloo which is an unbeatable dish made from dasheen leaves, ochroes (otherwise okra, or ladies' fingers), pig's tail, crab, coconut milk and the inevitable green pepper, all of which go into the pot to be boiled to the consistency of a thick soup. Calaloo and crab is one of Trinidad's most famous dishes. Served with stewed chicken and pounded plantain, it is as necessary to Sunday lunch as the Englishman's roast beef and Yorkshire pudding.

Plantain, incidentally, is like a much larger banana and is used as a vegetable, not as a fruit. When ripe it is usually

* The result of this dependence on root vegetables can be observed all over the Caribbean. Even those people who can afford a varied diet still tend to tuck into more starch than the weight-conscious European or American would think wise. Eds.

** Sancoche: probably derived from the Spanish *sincocho*, a similar dish made without pork (as its name states) — and sometimes, in its more frugal form, without any meat at all. Eds.

boiled or fried; when green, it is boiled and pounded to the consistency of creamed potatoes — and is delicious.

As well as liking hot and spicy food, Trinidadians have a sweet tooth. Visitors should try to get a taste of such delicacies as chip-chip, guava cheese, preserved citrus peel, tooloom (made of grated coconut, molasses and sugar) and sugar cake (grated coconut and sugar again, pressed into balls). The last two were first made by the African slaves, who required a great deal of energy for their arduous tasks and who were therefore, naturally, always hungry for sweet things.

The British arrived in 1797 and immediately began importing food from their own country. The fact that they were now living in a tropical country did not alter their eating habits. They brought in breakfast porridges and jams, jellies and marmalade such as they had been accustomed to — a pattern which continued for years. Indeed, it was only recently that we began to produce our own marmalades and jellies on a commercial scale, and this in a country where fruit grows abundantly.

It was the British who introduced the breadfruit (inspired in this case not by nostalgia but by a wish to grow a cheap food for their slaves). No Creole family worthy of the name would be without a breadfruit tree in the backyard. It is as handsome as it is useful: a tall flowering tree with magnificent foliage, bearing a large green fruit which can be boiled roasted, fried, stewed, and served in soups. It is said that when Captain Bligh of the *Bounty* met with his famous mutiny, he was on his way from the East Indies to the West Indies, bringing young breadfruit plants, and that he was more concerned with the plants than he was with his crew, denying the latter water in order to keep the former alive.

The emancipation of the slaves in the 1830s also had its effect on eating habits. Many of the slaves refused to work on the sugar plantations and had to find other means of earning a living. One thing most of them could do, and that was cook; so cook they did, setting up cook-shops on street corners. The shop was usually an old box with a charcoal fire on which they made souse and black pudding. It was in many ways the beginning of the itinerant café trade.

Later akra and float and cassava pone, coconut bread, and corn, joined the side-walk menu.

But there was yet another effect of emancipation. Refusal of the Africans to work left plantation owners without labour. They turned to India and recruited large numbers of indentured workers who began arriving in 1845, bringing their own food customs. Principal among these was the widespread use of curry seasoning and the famous roti. Both curry and roti have taken their place naturally in the national cuisine. The staple diet of Indians was rice and they planted it for use in their own homes and for sale to the Africans. Today rice is an essential part of the national diet, the basic ingredient of dishes such as pelau (rice with pigeon peas, meat and raisins), and 'peas and rice', two very, very Creole dishes.

The Chinese who settled here and started shops and laundries soon found that the rest of the community was looking with interest at their food, so it wasn't long before they were opening restaurants and capitalizing on the Trinidadian's keenness on food. The taste for Chinese food was quickly acquired and chow-mein is today in many homes a meal as common as pelau.

The trees of Trinidad are beautiful and bountiful bearers of delicious fruit whose names are as exotic as their flavours. There is the coconut and it is not for nothing that it is known as the nectar of the gods. The green nut produces a sweet, cool water. As the nut matures it produces a delicious soft jelly. When the nut grows to full strength it becomes hard and is then grated for use in cooking generally and for making sweets.

Then there are other fruits — the cashew, the nut of which is internationally known; papaw, soursop, guava, pomerac, mango, star-apple, sapodilla, and a wide variety of citrus fruit including grapefruit, oranges and tangerines.

The Caribbean is full of tales of pirates and the pirate and rum association is a strong one, strengthened by Robert Louis Stevenson who in *Treasure Island* scared us to death with his:

Fifteen men on the dead man's chest
Yo-ho-ho and a bottle of rum ....

The pirates have gone, but rum continues to give its rare warmth to the body. Trinidadians take it either 'straight', chased with water, or in drinks in which the taste of rum is always predominant. Of these the most famous is rum punch, made with rum, lime juice, syrup and grated nutmeg.

But rum is by no means the only thing we drink in these parts. In the old days, alcohol was forbidden to the slaves, so other refreshments had to be found for them. Thus it was that mauby (brewed from the bark of the mauby tree), ginger beer (from the ginger root) and sorrel (brewed from the flowering bud of the sorrel tree) came into use.

Visitors to Trinidad today can enjoy any of these Creole dishes and drinks that have come about a result of the interplay of Amerindian, European, African and Oriental influences.

From them all the colourful cooking of Trinidad takes its shape — spicy, enticing and exotic.

For the Tourist's Information

Up-to-date information on hotels and guest-houses, restaurants, sightseeing, etc, is readily available from the offices of the Tourist Board and from BWIA (British West Indian Airlines) at the following addresses:

Port of Spain

Trinidad & Tobago Tourist Board
56 Frederick Street
P.O. Box 222
Port of Spain
Trinidad, W.I

BWIA
Sunjet House
30 Edward Street
Port of Spain
Trinidad, W.I

BWIA
Kent House
Long Circular Road
Maraval
Port of Spain
Trinidad, W.I

London

Tourist Section
High Commissioner's Office
42 Belgrave Square
London SW1X 8NT

BWIA
16 Maddox Street
Mayfair,
London W.1

New York

Trinidad & Tobago Tourist Board
Suites 712-14
400 Madison Avenue
New York, N.Y. 10017

BWIA
Rockefeller Centre
610 Fifth Avenue
New York, N.Y. 10020

Orlando

Trinidad & Tobago Tourism and
Trade Centre (Suite 220)
807 West Morse Boulevard
Winter Park
Florida 32789

BWIA
Columbus Hotel
320 N.E. First Street
Miami, Florida 33132

Toronto

Trinidad & Tobago Tourist Board
Suite 1802
110 Yonge Street
Toronto 105
Canada

BWIA
44 King Street West
Suite 1219
Toronto 111
Canada

HOW TO GET THERE. There is a wide variety of flight services to Trinidad and Tobago. From the United Kingdom: BRITISH AIRWAYS and BWIA; From the USA: BWIA, EASTERN, PAA; From Canada: AIR CANADA, BWIA; From Continental Europe: KLM, SAS; From South America: BWIA, KLM, LAV and VIASA.

Passenger services by sea are available from the United Kingdom and Europe by COMPAÑIA ESPAÑIOLA. Limited passenger service aboard freight vessels is also available. From the USA: by freight vessels of ALCOA.

INTER-ISLAND TRAVEL. It is easy to visit the rest of the Caribbean from Trinidad and Tobago — LIAT runs a frequent scheduled inter-island air service (Room 2, First Floor, Salvatori Building, Frederick Street, Port of Spain, Trinidad, W.I). There are frequent daily flights between Piarco Airport, Trinidad, and Crown Point Airport, Tobago. Trinidad & Tobago Air Services, Sunjet House, 30 Edward Street, Port of Spain.

Sea transport between Trinidad and Tobago is provided by two boats, the *Scarlet Ibis* and the *Bird of Paradise*, which leave five or six times a week from the St Vincent Street jetty and which carry up to thirty-two cars. These boats are comfortable and inexpensive, but bad sailors are warned that the journey takes approximately six hours and choppy seas are often encountered.

For the rest, here are a few items of information which may be useful.

LANGUAGE. English — though some French patois, Spanish, Chinese, Hindi and Urdu are spoken.

DOCUMENTATION. Passports are required of all visitors. A valid smallpox vaccination certificate is also required (except citizens of the USA and its associated territories arriving therefrom).

CUSTOMS AND EXCISE. Visitors' personal belongings are duty-free with the following exceptions (for adults): there is a duty on liquor in excess of 1 quart and on tobacco in excess of 200 cigarettes or 50 cigars or ½ lb of tobacco.

CURRENCY. The Trinidad and Tobago (TT) dollar comes in coins of 1 cent, 5 cents, 10 cents, 25 cents and 50 cents, and bills of $ 1, $ 5, $ 10, and $ 20. Exchange rates are subject to fluctuation.

CLIMATE. Mean temperatures are 84°F by day and 74°F by night for a mean annual temperature of 79°F. The dry season is from January to May; the wet season is from June to December (showers are usually of short duration and are followed by brilliant sunshine, but the humidity can be oppressive). Treat the sun with respect — it is easy to get badly burnt.

CLOTHING. Only the lightest summer clothing is necessary, and informality is the general rule. Comfortable footwear is always important in a hot climate, and is doubly so if you come for Carnival and intend to jump-up.

ELECTRICITY. 115 volts 60 cycles AC.

DRIVING. Drive on the left. Valid UK, US and Canadian licences are accepted. Signs are in miles. Petrol (gas) is sold by the Imperial Gallon. Unless otherwise indicated, there is a 30 mph speed limit throughout Trinidad and Tobago (no hardship because the roads, though reasonably good, are twisty), and in neither Trinidad nor Tobago should you expect orthodox hand-signals from local traffic.

TAXES. Each visitor is charged $ 1.00 TT Emigration Tax on departure. Airline passengers pay an additional $ 1.00 Airport Tax when they check in for their flights. Cruise passengers who are on shore for less than forty-eight hours are not taxed.

ANIMALS. It is not recommended to bring in pets; entry requirements are very stringent and there is a six-month quarantine.

SHOPPING. Stores are open from 8.00 or 8.30 a.m. to 4.00 or 4.30 p.m. Monday through Thursday; 8.00 or 8.30 a.m. to 6.00 p.m. on Friday, and close at noon on Saturday — except for liquor and food stores which are open all day Saturday and close at noon on Thursday. There are some duty-free shops for visitors, which means that you get a receipt for your purchases and pick them up at the Customs Office at the dock or airport on your departure. In the supermarkets you will find much the same range of household goods, cosmetics, etc, as you would find at home.

BANKS. Banks are open from 8.00 a.m. to 12.30 p.m. Monday through Thursday and from 8.00 a.m. to 12.00 noon and 3.30 p.m. to 5.30 p.m. on Fridays.

Suggestions for Further Reading

Allen, R.P: *Birds of the Caribbean*, Viking Press, New York, 1961

Anthony, Michael: *The Games were Coming,* André Deutsch, London, 1963

Anthony, Michael: *Green Days by the River,* André Deutsch, London, 1967

Anthony, Michael: *The Year in San Fernando,* André Deutsch, London, 1965

Barcant, M: *The Butterflies of Trinidad and Tobago*, Collins, London, 1970

Boissière, Ralph de: *Crown Jewel*, Paul List Verlag, Leipzig, 1956

Bryans, Robin: *Trinidad and Tobago: isles of immortelles*, Faber, London, 1967

De Suze, José A: *New Trinidad and Tobago:* 14th ed., Collins, London, 1965

ffrench, Richard: *A Guide to the Birds of Trinidad and Tobago,* Livingstone Publishing Co, Wynnewood, Penn., USA, 1973

Herklots, G.A.C: *The Birds of Trinidad and Tobago*, Collins, London, 1961

Herskovits, Melville J. & Frances, S.: *Trinidad Village,* Octagon Books, New York, 1964

Hill, Errol: *Trinidad Carnival: Mandate for a National Theatre,* University of Texas Press, Austin, Texas, 1972

Hodge, Merle: *Crick Crack Monkey*, André Deutsch, London, 1970

Holder, Geoffrey with Harshman, Tom: *Black Gods, Green Islands*, Doubleday, New York, 1959

James, C.L.R.: *Beyond a Boundary,* Hutchinson, London, 1963

James, C.L.R.: *Minty Alley*, New Beacon, London, 1971

Joseph, Edward L.: *History of Trinidad*, Frank Cass, London, 1970

Khan, Ismith: *The Jumbie Bird*, MacGibbon & Kee, London, 1961

Kirkpatrick, T. W.: *Insect Life in the Tropics*, Longmans, Green & Co., London, 1957

Klass, Sheila: *Everyone in this House Makes Babies*, Doubleday, New York, 1964

LaBorde, Harold: *An Ocean to Ourselves*, Davies, London, 1960, Key Publishers, Trinidad, 1973

Leigh-Fermor, Patrick: *Traveller's Tree: a journey through the Caribbean Islands,* Murray & Co., London, 1950

Lewis, Enid: *Voices of Earth*, Rilloprint, Trinidad, 1972

Lovelace, Earl: *The Schoolmaster*, Collins, London, 1968

Mc Donald, Ian: *The Humming-bird Tree,* Heinemann, London, 1969

Naipaul, V.S.: *A House for Mr Biswas*, André Deutsch, London, 1961

Naipaul, V.S.: *The Loss of El Dorado*, André Deutsch, 1969

Naipaul, V.S.: *The Middle Passage: the Caribbean revisited*, André Deutsch, London, 1962

Naipaul, V.S.: *The Mimic Men*, André Deutsch, London, 1967

Naipaul, V.S.: *Miguel Street*, André Deutsch, London, 1959

Naipaul, V.S.: *The Mystic Masseur*, André Deutsch, London, 1957

Naipaul, V.S.: *The Suffrage of Elvira*, André Deutsch, London, 19

Naipaul, Shiva: *Fireflies,* André Deutsch, 1971

Naipaul, Shiva: *The Chip-Chip Gatherers,* André Deutsch, 1973

Patrick-Jones, Marion: *Pan Beat,* Columbus Publishers, Trinidad, 1973

Sanderson, I.T.: *Caribbean Treasure*, Hamish Hamilton, London, 1940

Selvon, Samuel: *A Brighter Sun*, Allan Wingate, London, 1952

Selvon, Samuel: *The Plains of Caroni*, McGibbon & Kee, London, 1970

Selvon, Samuel: *Those who Eat the Cascadura*, Davis-Poynter, London, 1972

Selvon, Samuel: *Ways of Sunlight,* Cunningham, London, 1957

Stewart, John: *Last Cool Days,* André Deutsch, London, 1971

Williams, Eric: *From Columbus to Castro: The History of the Caribbean*, André Deutsch, London, 1970

Williams, Eric: *History of the People of Trinidad and Tobago*, P.N.M. Publishing Co. Ltd., London, 1962, Deutsch, London, 1964

Williams, Eric: *Inward Hunger: the Education of a Prime Minister*, André Deutsch, London, 1969

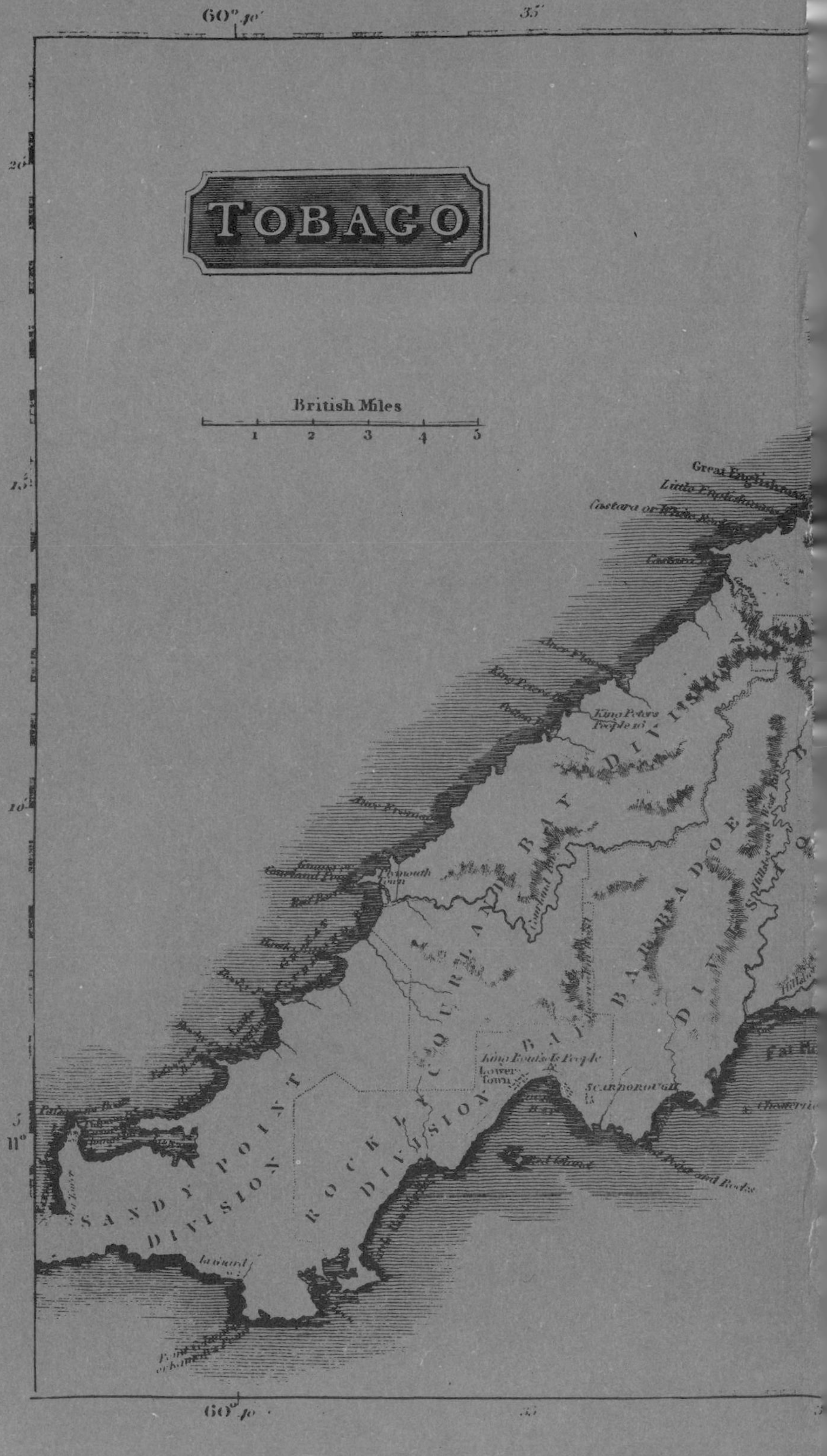

60° 40'
35'
20'
15'
10'
5
11°
TOBAGO
British Miles
1 2 3 4 5
King Peters People
Plymouth Town
SANDY POINT DIVISION
ROCKLY DIVISION
COURLAND BAY DIVISION
BARBADOES DIVISION
Lower Town
SCARBOROUGH